TRY
READING THE BIBLE
THIS WAY

TRY
READING THE BIBLE THIS WAY

by
Raymond E. Balcomb

THE WESTMINSTER PRESS
Philadelphia

Scripture quotations from the Revised Standard
Version of the Bible are copyright, 1946 and 1952,
by the Division of Christian Education of the National Council of Churches, and are used by permission.

ISBN 664-0-24924-8

LIBRARY OF CONGRESS CATALOG CARD No. 76-153866

Grateful acknowledgment is made to the following publishers
for permission to use their copyrighted materials:

Burnes & Oates, Ltd., for the first stanza from "The Hound
of Heaven," by Francis Thompson.

The Macmillan Company, for lines from "Epitaph," in *Collected Poems,* by Thomas Hardy. Copyright 1925 by The
Macmillan Company.

W. W. Norton & Company, Inc., for lines from a poem in
Hands Laid Upon the Wind, by Bonaro W. Overstreet. Copyright 1955 by W. W. Norton & Company, Inc.

Book design by Dorothy Alden Smith

Published by The Westminster Press ®

Philadelphia, Pennsylvania

PRINTED IN THE UNITED STATES OF AMERICA

This is for J.B. Balcomb
who practices Biblical religion
in his daily life
while others talk about it

CONTENTS

FOREWORD

I ONCE HEARD of a man who set out with great determination to read the Bible. He began at the beginning, which would seem logical, and applied himself with diligence. He was confronted at the outset, of course, with an account of Creation which, so far as he could tell, he was meant to accept as a straightforward description. He tried, even though it conflicted with most of what he thought he had been taught about geology and biology. His incredulity mounted, however, as he read of a snake that talked, about five-hundred-year-old men who fathered children, about a boat that held either two or seven of every kind of animal. He persevered until he came to the passage which said that God once made the sun stand still in order to give his favorites more daylight in which to complete the wanton slaughter of a people fighting in self-defense. Then he balked. He couldn't take it anymore. He was willing to try to reconcile scientific discrepancies, but not moral ones. He didn't want to have anything to do with a bloodthirsty war god. "I've given up Bible-reading," he told a friend. "I found it was undermining my faith."

This book is for people who have had similar experiences, people who have wondered and hoped that the Bible has something of value for them, and for us all, but who have never quite been able to find it. It is a book that deals with some of the most famous passages in the Bible, and some of the less famous; it deals with some of the hardest passages and some of the easiest. It is based on the predominant trends in Biblical scholarship of the last hundred years, and tries to show how such scholarship has increased the value of the Bible for us, yet it does not insist on any particular interpretations. It hopes only to open a few windows for those who have been in a great darkness, and to stimulate all to read the Book more faithfully and with greater insight and appreciation.

The cry of the times is for church renewal. Every renewal of the church has been stimulated by a resurgence of Biblical knowledge. Perhaps this little book can help toward that end in our time.

I thank Mrs. Burton Bastuscheck for her typing assistance.

R. E. B.

Chapter 1

THE POOR MAN'S WISDOM

IN A COLLEGE TOWN I picked up a copy of the student-staffed university daily newspaper. On its front page was a striplike cartoon of a man thinking:

If you are a political person / and do not study history / your politics will provoke chaos, anarchy and repression. / If you are a political person and study history / your politics will provoke disillusion, apathy and cynicism. / So the question is: / Whether to ignore history and be jailed— / or learn its lessons and be impotent. / What a choice.

I have no way of knowing how representative that is of student thinking these days, but I do know that it bears some striking resemblances to the book of Ecclesiastes. It has some of the same attitude of resigned realism, the same brand of humor and irony, the same reflective spirit, the same shocking unconventionality, the same feeling of futility and frustration, which are such marked characteristics of Ecclesiastes.

Ecclesiastes has a great deal to say to us. Not long ago a young person wrote to me: "Where in the Bible will

you find a passage commanding man 'to raise his head
and find joy in his own being; to live purely for the
sake of life.' " It was not asked as a question; it was
made as an unanswerable criticism. "Where do you find
a passage that tells a man to be proud that he is a man;
to stand up and face the world—*by standing on his own
two feet.*" That, I would judge, is not an isolated attitude, but one rather common among people under
thirty. Fortunately it was an easy note to answer—I just
referred the writer to Ecclesiastes (and the commentary
on it by Robert Gordis, *Koheleth—The Man and His
World*). Ecclesiastes is a book for times like ours! Beneath the surface of its apparent cynicism, pessimism,
and determinism there is a candor and an honesty which
is refreshing. Few books, if any, in the Bible come
closer to "telling it like it is" (which, of course, is only
as it appears to be to the observer at the moment), and
then drawing thoughtful and reflective, rather than
merely emotional, conclusions. Ecclesiastes is the

> cry of a sensitive spirit wounded by man's cruelty
> and ignorance, . . . [the] distilled essence of an
> honest and courageous mind, striving to penetrate
> the secret of the universe. . . . One of man's
> noblest offerings on the altar of truth.[1]

Let us begin our examination of what it has to say
to us by focusing on that brief passage which tells a story
or a parable about a small city that was besieged by a
great king (Eccl. 9:13 to 10:1). The odds were all against
the small city, "but there was found in it a poor wise
man, who saved the city by his wisdom." To the story
itself the author adds some generally accepted proverbs
and then counters each by another of his own.

I

One of the things, obviously, which this is saying is that *the high and the mighty do well at times to listen to the poor*. He doesn't say how this "poor wise man" saved the city, but it is plain that the man wasn't a member of the local power structure. No one built any monuments to him afterward, either—no one even remembered him! His wisdom saved the city, but his poverty prevented any recognition.

That has happened more than once in history. Compared to the high and mighty cardinals and popes, Martin Luther was only a poor wise man. Until very recent times it seems that most of them have been trying to erase his memory from the mind of man. But the scholars now are pointing out that

> Luther saved the papacy. . . . The See of Peter in the age of the Renaissance was on the way toward becoming a secularized Italian city-state. If that process had not been arrested the result for the papacy would have been far more drastic than anything which did happen. A secularized Italian city-state would not have continued to command the obedience of the nations, nor even of the other Italian city-states. Luther revived the religious consciousness of Europe. Luther was responsible for the calling of the council of Trent. The popes persistently opposed the calling of a council lest their wings be clipped.[2]

Compared to the high and the mighty like Caiaphas and Pilate, Jesus was only a poor wise man. Do you remember that terrible word which Luke records?

And when he drew near and saw the city he wept
over it, saying, "Would that even today you knew
the things that make for peace! But now they are
hid from your eyes. For the days shall come upon
you, when your enemies will cast up a bank about
you and surround you, and hem you in on every
side, and dash you to the ground, you and your
children within you, and they will not leave one
stone upon another in you; because you did not
know the time of your visitation." (Luke 19:41–44.)

And that, of course, is exactly what happened to Jerusalem in A.D. 70.

Surely it is not stretching the parallel to say that we
are like a city besieged: the great king Communism has
boasted that it will bury us; the great king of hunger
and want among most of the world's people stares greed-
ily at our affluence; the great king color reminds us that
we are but a shrinking fraction of the population of the
globe. In my judgment, men like Malcolm X, Stokely
Carmichael, and Bobby Seale are some of the poor wise
men of our time. And we, the high and the mighty (even
though we think of ourselves as only the middle class),
would do well to hear what they have to say. We have
had gigantic demonstrations on Vietnam and other social problems. So far they have seldom deteriorated into
destructive mobs. Granted, they do not represent "the
silent majority." The point is that we will be foolish in
the extreme if we stubbornly insist that we will not
listen in any degree to what they are saying. To some
they look like Communist revolutionaries. Well, does
anyone think that the czars in Russia were toppled because they weren't repressive enough? Because they were
too democratic or bent over backward too far to be just?
These could be the poor wise men who would save our

city if we would only listen to what they are saying before it is too late.

A second thing this parable of the poor man's wisdom
says is that *"wisdom is better than might"* (Eccl. 9:16).
The wisdom of the poor man was better than the might
—whatever it was—of the conventional defenders of
the city. It was even better than the overwhelming might
of the aggressor.

I once heard "power" defined as "the ability to
achieve purpose." It is a good definition. Sheer physical
might is not necessarily power. In this parable, wisdom
proves to be more powerful—that is, better able to
achieve the desired purpose—than "all the king's horses
and all the king's men."

Wisdom is better than might. No one has ever accused Woody Hayes, the Ohio State football coach, of
despising might. His teams make a habit of winning;
they have won two out of three in the Rose Bowl. In
this age of passers he says that he likes the old-fashioned
off-tackle power play for just one reason: "It wins." Yet,
when Woody goes recruiting, he does not look only at
the size of the boy, or his speed, or his ability.

> We concentrate on character. We talk to their
> parents, their teachers, their principals, coaches,
> ministers, priests. If a kid doesn't have character,
> you don't have a chance.[3]

> I can spot that good home as soon as I walk in the
> door. I don't mean the furnishings and the money.
> I mean whether a kid is loved and whether there
> is discipline in the home.[4]

And when his team lost a game and its number-one rank-
ing one year, Woody, who is not known as a good loser,

had the wisdom and character to say, "We were out-fought, outplayed, outcoached."

Wisdom is better than might. We would do well to keep that in mind in trying to steer a course through our troubled era. I was glad when I heard the President say that he at first thought the answer to marijuana was just tougher law enforcement, but now he thinks it is more a problem of helping youth to understand its dangers and to show them the advantages of the straight society. The religious and social upheaval of our time is turning out to be more dark and stormy than the Reformation was, and some advice the great Christian Erasmus gave then to the pope about dealing with the Lutherans is all the more germane to us:

> Some would advise you to cure this malady by toughness. This course would be very imprudent and might end in frightful slaughter. If the proper method to eradicate this evil be prisons, floggings, confiscations, exiles, censures, and executions you have no need of my counsel. . . . First you should try to discover how this evil arose. Offer immunity to those who were seduced by others. Better still offer a general amnesty. If God daily pardons the contrite should his vicar do anything else? The suppression of innovations by the magistrates leads not to piety but to sedition.[5]

The pope didn't follow the advice—and the result was a whole century of violence and bloodshed. Wisdom is better than might.

Let us now move a surprising step farther: *it is a wise man who is alert to the inadequacies of his own class and his own system*. Ecclesiastes is part of Israel's "wisdom" literature; that is a technical classification just as "poetry" and "prophecy" and "law" are technical literary classifications. Its author was a professional wise man, a teacher of wisdom, and a fairly affluent one, at that. He was in Israel what the philosopher was in Greece or the theologian in medieval Europe or the scientist is to us. And *the surprising thing about him is that he recognized the limitations of wisdom.* That is what those antithetical proverbs mean which he has joined to his parable. "Wisdom is better than might," yes, but wisdom isn't everything. It doesn't overcome every obstacle: "the poor man's wisdom is despised" (Eccl. 9:16) and is thus ineffective!

> It is said, "The words of the wise spoken quietly are heard better than the ranting of the king of fools," and "wisdom is better than weapons"; but I say, "One fool can destroy much good," and "As dying flies befoul the perfumer's ointment, so a little folly can outweigh an abundance of wisdom." (Eccl. 9:17 to 10:1, Gordis tr.)

How much we need to remember our own inadequacies! Dean Acheson, Secretary of State at the time of the Korean War, says that a military victory in Korea was changed into a military stalemate chiefly because General MacArthur was too sure of his own genius and invulnerability. After the Inchon landing he turned what had been a small-scale action into a full-blown war by ignoring warnings from Washington about the probability of Chinese military response, and those thousands of "volunteers" swarming across the Yalu River shattered his ego as well as his army. "A little folly can outweigh an abundance of wisdom."

We need to remember our own inadequacies and the inadequacies of our own system. The wise man needs to recognize the limitations of wisdom, the preacher the

limitations of religion, the demonstrator the limitations
of confrontation politics, the lawyer the limitations of
the law, the scientist the limitations of science, the citizen the limitations of patriotism. As Michael Novak, the
Roman Catholic philosopher, reminded us a while back:

> We habitually believe that American intentions are
> good ones, that America has never started a war,
> that America is always on the side of democracy and
> justice and liberty, that Americans are unusually in-
> nocent, generous and good in their relationships
> with other people.[6]

All our judgments are fallible, and perhaps particularly
those about ourselves. The massacres in Vietnam show
that a generation of militarism brutalizes us as much as
anyone else. It is now apparent that our CIA has gone
far beyond espionage into political subversion and assassination—things completely at odds with our basic
national ideals and moral principles.

There is a statue of Oliver Cromwell outside the halls
of Parliament in London. As I looked at it I remembered that he had once said something like this to the
opposition before going into battle: "I beseech you in
the bowels of Christ to think it possible that you may
be mistaken." It must be admitted that there were times
when it would have been well if Cromwell had followed
that advice himself! But it must also be admitted that
it was he who laid down in law for the first time a principle of religious toleration. As staunch a Puritan as he
was, he had at least a glimmer of a realization that his
own system might be inadequate.

Were the author of Ecclesiastes living now, I see no
reason why he would be optimistic. On most important
fronts—population, pollution, war, poverty, race—the

world seems to be losing rather than gaining ground. I think, rather, that he might concur with the chaplain of Yale University:

> I am not optimistic, but I *am* hopeful. . . . Realism demands pessimism. But hope demands that we take a dim view of the present because we hold a bright view of the future; and hope arouses, as nothing else can arouse, a *passion for the possible*.[7]

Ecclesiastes is of everlasting value, then, because it tackles a problem that plagues us all, at least at times: Is life worth living? Most of us have times when we wonder! I will never forget hearing one of America's great men say that he once went to get a razor to cut his own throat. More people have thought of suicide than this world dreams of. "Whoever has dreamt great dreams in his youth and seen the vision flee, or has loved and lost, or has beaten barehanded at the fortress of injustice and come back bleeding and broken, has passed Koheleth's door and tarried awhile beneath the shadow of his roof." [8]

Let's move on to look at what these somewhat disconnected reflections of the voice of experience have to say to us about life.

II

The book of Ecclesiastes says that we are tragically ignorant about life. "As you do not know how the spirit comes to the bones in the womb of a woman with child," it says, "so you do not know the work of God who makes everything" (Eccl. 11:5). Really, in the last analysis, we are ignorant—tragically ignorant—of what is going on.

John Dewey, the late famous and influential American

philosopher and educator, would stand at the blackboard and draw a line with an arrow on each end. What
he meant by that was that "the universe is open at both
ends." We don't know where we came from and we
don't know where we're going. We just know we're here.
That is Koheleth's idea exactly.

We are ignorant, moreover, of even our mortal future.
One of the prayers in the funeral ritual of the church begins with these words: "Eternal God, who committest
to us the swift and solemn trust of life: since we know
not what a day may bring forth but only that the hour
for serving Thee is always present, may we wake to the
instant claims of Thy holy will." Surely that is our condition. We do not know what a day may bring forth; we
are tragically ignorant of the future.

Furthermore, we are also ignorant of ultimate truth.
The average modern is of course ready at once to acknowledge that we have no ultimate standard in philosophy or religion. But it is a shock to realize that even in
science there are few if any absolutes. We usually regard
mathematics as a sort of infallible revealer of absolute
truth. Do you remember how you learned to "prove"
theorems in geometry? It has been a long time since I
looked into a geometry book, but unless I am mistaken,
there were something like eleven axioms that we learned.
On them all our proofs rested. But did anyone ever
prove an axiom? No. We assumed them. And Euclidean
geometry, while useful and handy here, does not hold
true in interstellar space.

Dorothy Day has a fine passage in her autobiography
in which she suggests that no preacher ever goes into the
pulpit without promulgating heresy. What she means is
that the truth is so pure, so holy, so vast, that we never
see it whole. We always understate some part of it in

order to make another part plain. No scientist ever forms a hypothesis that doesn't do violence to truth; no musician ever pens a score that doesn't do violence to harmony; no artist ever touches a brush to a canvas that doesn't do violence to beauty; no dramatist or novelist ever writes that doesn't do violence to life. We never fully know the absolutes. We are tragically ignorant about life.

Then again, *the book of Ecclesiastes says that a realistic view of life must include evil as well as good.* "In my vain life," says Koheleth, "I have seen everything; there is a righteous man who perishes in his righteousness, and there is a wicked man who prolongs his life in his evil-doing." (Eccl. 7:15.)

There is a very persistent idea in religious circles that the righteous prosper and the wicked suffer. Two hundred and fifty years ago Cotton Mather, the New England Puritan historian, wrote: "Let the ark be in the town, and God will bless the town! I believe it may be found, that in the mortal scourges of heaven which this town has felt, there has been a *discernible* distinction of those that have come up to attend all the ordinances of the Lord Jesus Christ in the communion of his churches." And he notes that "some very judicious persons have observed, that as 'they sanctify the Lord's Day, remissly or carefully, just so their affairs usually prospered all the ensuing week.'" About a generation later a man by the name of Henry Fielding was writing an even more famous book, one that has been made into a notable movie, *Tom Jones*. And in the book, which was written "to recommend goodness and innocence," Fielding points out that

> there are a set of religious, or rather moral writers, who teach that virtue is the certain road to hap-

piness, and vice to misery, in this world. A very wholesome and comfortable doctrine, and to which we have but one objection, namely, that it is not true.[9]

Well, Fielding was a more realistic observer of human life than Cotton Mather, and Koheleth agrees with Fielding. Good people do not necessarily have fewer troubles than evil people. The race is not—as it ought to be—always to the swift, nor the battle to the strong, nor riches to the honest, nor good fortune to the godly! "Time and chance happen to them all." (Eccl. 9:11.)

As a simple moralism will not do, so neither will the idea that evil is wholly illusory.

My friend, there is no suffering—to think so is to sin,
Remember you are God's child, and let His presence
    in.
Since God is All, forever, what is there to heal?
God surely cannot suffer, and matter cannot feel.
With truth and goodness present, how then can
    sickness stay?
For good is never evil, as night is never day.
So when you think you're suffering (which really
    you are not),
The cure is very simple—just change your sinful
    thought.[10]

It makes a lovely sound, but that bit of doggerel has never said very much to me because it was given me— with a smile—by an earnest and consecrated Christian woman who had been painfully bedridden for more than twenty years! Ecclesiastes is right. One's view of life must take in the reality of evil as well as good.

One of the late Ernest Hemingway's best stories was *The Old Man and the Sea*. It is a yarn about an old fisherman who, after a long spell of no luck, finally out-fights a huge fish. But even after the long-deserved victory he loses, because sharks rip his prize to shreds before he can get it home. With clean-cut artistry Hemingway has caught a fragment of life with its mysterious and inexplicable twists, its evil entwined with its good.

Evil, misfortune, suffering, injustice are all a part of human experience. One's view of life must neither wink at them nor dodge them. They must be accepted.

The book of Ecclesiastes also reminds us that life is to be enjoyed. This realistic man, who was wise enough to know that we are all tragically ignorant of the final issues of life and who was clear-eyed enough to see and admit the evil in life, nevertheless was sure that life was well worth living. It is to be enjoyed. "It is God's gift to man that every one should eat and drink and take pleasure in his toil," he says. (Eccl. 3:13.) He would have agreed with Jackie Gleason, "How sweet it is!" He would have agreed with Washington Gladden's judgment: "There may be better worlds than this but I should like to be guaranteed another seventy years in just such a world as this." "Light is sweet," says Koheleth, "and it is pleasant for the eyes to behold the sun. . . . If a man lives many years, let him rejoice in them all." (Ch. 11:7, 8.) For all its frustrations, disappointments, and inequities, life remains the central good in the world. Our Jewish friends read this book during the Feast of Tabernacles, the season of rejoicing.

I would not be misunderstood. Koheleth was no mere sensualist. He is no advocate of licentiousness or excess in any form. The enjoyments he recommends are the satisfactions of wholesome living—eat your bread with happiness, rejoice in life with the woman you love, give yourself to your work wholeheartedly.

There are still some who seem to think that the religious life is a matter of long faces and reserved, if not downright sanctimonious, behavior. But Jesus Christ our Lord was no such person! Little children flocked to him; would they be attracted to some who are accounted pillars in the church these days? He was called a friend of publicans and sinners—the socially and religiously outcast of his time; how long has it been since that kind of charge was made against any of us?

Jesus was called a glutton and a winebibber—slander, no doubt, yet still a testimony that he hardly took an ascetic view of life! When they asked him why his disciples didn't go in for fasting he said that life in his group was like one big wedding celebration! When one of the Gospelers came to tell of his birth, the best way he could say what he meant was to picture an angelic chorus singing "joy to the world!" And another of the Gospels tells us that he came that we might have life and have it abundantly! Can anyone imagine that Jesus would have given a negative answer to the question, Is life worth living? Would he not, too, say, "How sweet it is!"

There is a sense in which the Old Testament may be said to know the questions, while the New Testament has the answers. I think that is true of Ecclesiastes. Events have made possible for us a reasonable faith in immortality, in our origin and destiny which Koheleth never had. But if he lacked the note of certainty that right would triumph, he at least believed that it should. He is a reminder yet that some ills cannot be transformed but must be transcended. And he calls us all to face this "incomprehensible and indescribably precious blessing called life" with truth as our banner and with a song in our hearts!

III

One of the most moving scenes in the famous novel *Moby Dick* comes on the day before the great white whale is finally sighted. "It was a clear steel-blue day," warm and mild, and Captain Ahab, leaning over the rail, is in a rare pensive mood. The chief mate, Starbuck, quietly joins him. They fall to talking about their homes and families, and Starbuck tries to get his captain to forget his vengeful search and turn for home. But Ahab is under compulsion, and he asks:

> Is Ahab, Ahab? Is it I, God, or who, that lifts this arm? But if the great sun move not of himself, but is an errand boy in heaven, no one single star can revolve but by some invisible power, how then can this one small heart beat, this one small brain think . . . unless God does that beating, does that thinking, does that living, and not I. By heaven, man, we are turned round and round in this world, like yonder windlass, and Fate is the handspike.[11]

Is there anyone who hasn't wondered, at least once in a while, about his own freedom to choose and to do? Anyone who hasn't wondered whether or not "we are turned round and round in this world" like a windlass, with Fate doing the turning? Anyone who has not wondered at the compulsions that sometimes drive him?

A few months ago I was at a meeting with about twenty colleagues from the western part of the country. Most of us flew to and from the meeting via the Los Angeles International Airport. Following the meeting, one of the group was on a plane that disintegrated in the air shortly after takeoff. Was it just by chance that only

he of our group was on that flight, while others going
to the same city were on another? Or was death "in the
cards" for him and not for us? Why has so much tragedy
dogged the talented Kennedy family? Why are there
those flukes in battle which spare one soldier's life and
take another's? There was a popular song years ago
which occasionally is still heard, *"Que será, será"* (Whatever will be, will be"), and who can look back over his
own life and not wonder how much truth there is in it?

It is not only ordinary people who cannot quite pin
down this problem. Even the ablest are perplexed by it.
You could almost write the history of philosophy, for
example, in terms of it. It is one of the watersheds in
Christian theology. Psychiatry has its own ambivalence:
classic psychoanalytic theory, on the one hand, is de-
terministic. "In the mind, as in physical nature about
us," we are told, "nothing happens by chance." There is
a strict law of cause and effect. A "Freudian slip" of the
tongue is not really a slip at all, but a revealing effect;
there is no such thing as "accidentally" mislaying your
glasses or "forgetting" an appointment! But Sigmund
Freud's successor in Vienna these days is stressing the
importance of "the will to live"! Historians, too, may
be divided into two schools: the "conspiracy" school,
which says that if something happened, somebody
planned it; and the "confusion" school, which believes
more in the "role of chance and contingency, the sheer
intricacy of situations, the murk of battle." Newtonian
physics was virtually based on causality, but now quan-
tum mechanics has found that subatomic particles dis-
play an "indeterminacy principle"—an element of ran-
domness or unpredictability!

The Bible, too, displays both kinds of thinking: free-
will, choice, responsibility on the one hand, and deter-

minism on the other. The third chapter of Ecclesiastes is unquestionably its most eloquent spokesman for pure determinism. "For everything there is a season, and a time for every matter under heaven" (Eccl. 3:1)—all earthly events are predetermined by God. Human actions, as well as natural events (Ahab's compulsive search for revenge as well as the rising of the sun), happen at the time and place foreordained by God, and we can neither understand nor change them. Koheleth (the pen name of the author, which by translation into Greek, Latin, and finally English comes out "Ecclesiastes") is not, however, as often charged, either a cynic or a pessimist. He does not believe that things are going from bad to worse, nor does he sneer at human motives. Rather, his book is written in a minor chord, so to speak; it has a mood of melancholy and sadness forced upon it by "the anomalies and mysteries of human life." What oppresses him most is that man is given no glimpse of the meaning of life: God has put eternity into our minds, yet in such a way that we "cannot find out what God has done from the beginning to the end" (Eccl. 3:11).

It must be said that neither Jews nor Christians, so far as the majority is concerned, have ever been willing to go all the way with Koheleth. But it is not likely that we will ever be able to forget him, either. There is something in this little poem that made it John F. Kennedy's favorite Bible passage. There is something in it which speaks to our time, and especially to the younger generation, as witness Pete Seeger's pop-folk song "Turn! Turn! Turn!" which is directly based on it. Let's look at a couple of things it brings to mind.

One of these is the implicit contention that *a healthy agnosticism is better than a sick piety*. Whatever else you say about Koheleth, you have to admire the clarity of his mind and the integrity of his spirit. He is neither naïve nor cynical; he is not a Pollyanna, nor is he a crepehanger. Like the author of Job, he is courageously attacking religious thinking which has become stereotyped and superficial; his work was so disturbing, in fact, that some orthodox soul has tried to patch up the last chapter with some conventional clichés!

It seems to me that a lot of the Christian piety in our time is sick. It is sick with sentimentality about "the old-time religion." It is sick with a bad infection of success pseudopsychology. It is sick with a scurvy resulting from a lack of ethical vitamins. It is sick with the delusion of separating "spiritual" matters from "business" or "politics." It is sick with institutional inertia. One of our popular magazines recently had a piece on the changes taking place in American Catholicism. On the whole, it felt that revolutionary changes were going to be effected successfully. But the embattled former priest James J. Kavanaugh took issue:

> Unfortunately, you missed the whole point of what is taking place. This is not another Lutheran rage of 95 theses, nor is it merely another thrust against a latter-day Pius IX. It is not even an introduction to the halfway house of Callahan, Curran and Company. It is the death of the church. The young people with whom I communicate do not want a reformed church, a free church or an open church. They don't want any church, because they have grown free enough, mature enough not to need it. They have the best of its values without its fears, its hang-ups, its commitment to . . . structures. They can live honestly in or out of community, deal with present poverty, suffering, injustice—without the church. The liberals who suggest a church with-

out compelling dogmas, stifling rituals and unreal
moral codes will find that such a church already
exists. It is called the world, and its adherents are
called men.[12]

That is strongly put! In fact, it probably overstates its
case, and I, for one, would say that there are some flaws
in its rhetoric. But my guess is that, iconoclastic and
agnostic as it sounds, it may be a good deal healthier
than a lot of the smothering piety which it is attacking.

The other thing that this third chapter of Ecclesiastes
brings to mind is that *life is deeper than logic.* Its author
was a wise and learned man; he has observed life and he
has reflected thoughtfully on what he has observed.
More than any other book in the Bible it seems to have
affinities with the kind of rational thought that made
Greece the home of philosophy. And, for sheer logic, his
pure determinism can hardly be faulted. He has a systematic and orderly and consistent way of looking at
life.

But, for all that, it does not quite satisfy us. It does
not really explain satisfactorily all the things we want
explained. It does not seem that we can be permanently
convinced that we live in such an iron-clad straitjacket.
Maybe you remember the story about the man newly
turned fatalist who refused to fly. "Why," said a fellow
fatalist, "if your time comes, you'll go whether you're in
a plane or not." "I know," said the novice, "but suppos-
ing I'm up with a pilot and *his* time comes?" Life always
turns out to be deeper, broader, more complex than any
of the systems to which we try to reduce it or by which
we try to define it.

A few years ago an English author by the name of
William Golding was the literary lion of the hour. A
book of his called *Lord of the Flies* had apparently had

a delayed-action fuse but had finally gone off with a bang. It was a story about human depravity—some well-bred English schoolboys who reverted to savagery. He followed it with another book called *The Spire*. And again his theme was the evil in "the given nature of man," shown this time by the harm done by a "good" man. The central character is the dean of a medieval English cathedral whose consuming ambition is to complete his cathedral with a magnificent spire. In the course of building it, he not only builds a spire on an insufficient foundation, he also ruins himself and almost everyone he touches. It is a powerful argument for the traditional Christian brand of determinism called "original sin."

But wait! History itself has written, perhaps, the sequel to Golding's tale. Since he grew up not far from the Salisbury Cathedral, and since a clergyman with the very same name as his "hero" is buried there, and since Salisbury has England's "tallest and loveliest spire," it seems fair to think that Golding got his idea there. That 400-foot real-life spire was built in the fourteenth century, and promptly settled twenty-three inches out of plumb. Visiting mechanical engineers have been seen to cross themselves because "there is no reason why it should stand." But for six hundred years the massive masonry with the inadequate foundation "has rested as safely as a marsh hen's egg on the watery sod"! Life is deeper than logic!

There is a true story about two Methodist professors of philosophy, Lorenzo Dow McCabe and Borden Parker Bowne. They were good friends, but McCabe held that if human freedom has any reality at all, it must be that the Almighty, in granting freedom to us, has thereby limited his foreknowledge to all our possible choices without any certainty as to what any particular choice might be. This was too subtle for many people and McCabe was unfairly accused of teaching "the ignorance of God." Bowne was unwilling to believe that God was limited in any way, even by a self-limitation. One evening, when Bowne was visiting McCabe, they fell to arguing. The debate went on until three A.M. The next morning, as Dr. Bowne left for his train, McCabe stood at the gate and called after him: "Bowne, do you think God could have created this world if he had seen how it was coming out?" To which the other promptly called back, "McCabe, do you think God could have created this world if he hadn't seen how it was coming out?" It may be that we'll never answer those questions to everyone's complete satisfaction! But we can be glad for, and profit from, Koheleth's unforgettable attempt.

Chapter 2

THE ANCIENT MARINER

BECAUSE THE BIBLE is a book of experience, the note of responsibility runs through it. One of the places it comes out most clearly is in the little Book of Jonah. Everyone has heard about "Jonah and the whale." Great storms of controversy have raged over it. Could a whale (or, more accurately, "a great fish") really swallow a man alive? And if it did, could the man live in its stomach for three days? I suggest you bypass all of that because it is irrelevant. It makes no difference whether Jonah is literal history or imaginative fiction or a combination of both. As with most of the Bible, if you start reading it as history, you will find that it is full of fiction. On the other hand, if you start reading it as fiction, you will find that it is full of history.

Jonah is not so much natural history as moral history. It is a parable that is meant to teach God's universal love, and in that respect it is a true forerunner of him who said that no sign would be given but the sign of Jonah (Luke 11:29). In the process it also says something about being responsive to responsibility, and it is about this incidental theme that I want to write now.

I

The first thing we see in it is this: *when you evade responsibility you are heading for trouble*. That's what happened to Jonah: "Now the word of the Lord came to Jonah . . . , saying, 'Arise, go to Nineveh, that great city, and cry against it. . . .' But Jonah rose to flee to Tarshish" (Jonah 1:1). Nineveh lay to the east of Palestine, but Tarshish lay to the west, clear over in Spain. Jonah set out to evade his responsibility by putting as much distance between it and himself as possible. But what happened? The ship and all aboard came close to disaster. When you try to evade responsibility you are heading for trouble.

The Bible puts that same word in a story called "Jotham's Fable" (Judg. 9:7-15). It was told when Israel's fortunes had sunk to a low ebb because its leadership was corrupt. So the old prophet made up a story about how the trees had once set out to find a king to rule over them. They offered the regal coronet first to the olive (which is the most important fruit tree in Palestine), but the olive was above getting involved. The fig tree also declined on the grounds that it was beneath its dignity. The vine argued that it was too busy making the wine that cheers to do the job. So, finally, the crown went to the bramble—a useless, fruitless bush good for nothing but burning. For noble and useful trees to be ruled by a bramble bush would be a sad absurdity. But, even worse, even the best of trees can be destroyed by a fire started in the brambles. So the prophet is saying that "when people shirk civic responsibilities, evil triumphs!"

You see it over and over again. The parent who evades the responsibility of inculcating religion in the home—

grace at the table, family prayers together, the regular reading of the Bible, a striving for justice and the practice of reconciliation—the parent who evades or neglects these things is heading for trouble. The man who works for a living, but who evades the responsibility of giving an honest day's work, who doesn't keep the business of his employer at the forefront of his mind, who thinks that the world owes him a living—that man is heading for trouble. The businessman or the farmer who directly or indirectly controls the jobs and the welfare of others, but who evades responsibility for human beings' right to decent living conditions, who looks with indifference on urban ghettos or rural migrant camps, who wants no minimum wages or social security or sanitary standards, is heading for trouble. The housewife who evades the responsibility for creating a cheerful and inviting atmosphere in her home is heading for trouble. When we evade responsibility we get into trouble.

But the story doesn't stop there. Another thing we can see in it is that *when we accept responsibility God will help us to fulfill it*. That's what happened to Jonah. When he came to his senses and realized that evasion meant trouble he resolved to do his duty. "What I have vowed I will pay" (Jonah 2:9), he said. And he went to Nineveh, with the result that he was one of the most phenomenally successful preachers imaginable. He changed the moral tone of the whole town, "from the greatest of them to the least of them" (Jonah 3:5). He even got through to the king himself!

There is a scene in the life of the ever self-confident Winston Churchill which almost takes you by surprise. It comes at the end of the day when he first took charge of the Admiralty before World War I. The Kaiser had already set the alarm bells ringing throughout Europe

by his gunboat diplomacy and Foreign Secretary Sir
Edward Grey had warned that "the Fleet might be attacked at any moment." As he went to bed that night
Churchill turned to the Bible. His mind was dominated
by the enormity of the task before him.

> I thought of the peril of Britain, peace loving, un-
> thinking, little prepared . . . and of her mission
> of good sense and fair play. I thought of mighty
> Germany, towering up in the splendour of her Im-
> perial State and delving down in her profound,
> cold, patient, ruthless calculations. . . . I opened
> the Book . . . and in the 9th Chapter of Deuteron-
> omy I read:
> "Hear, O Israel: Thou art to pass over Jordan this
> day, to go in to possess nations greater and mightier
> than thyself, cities great and fenced up to heaven.
> A people great and tall the children of the Anakim,
> whom thou knowest, and of whom thou hast heard
> say, 'Who can stand before the children of Anak!'
> Understand therefore this day, that the Lord thy
> God is he which goeth over before thee; as a con-
> suming fire he shall destroy them, and he shall
> bring them down before thy face; so shalt thou
> drive them out, and destroy them quickly, as the
> Lord hath said unto thee." [13]

It seemed a message full of reassurance. When you
accept a responsibility, God will help you to fulfill it!

Back when Palestine was still a British mandate and
the modern state of Israel had not even been created, a
Westerner was talking with a Jewish rabbi there about
that chronically inflamed situation. He asked whether
there was any way out and the rabbi answered that
there were just two ways out. "One is the natural way
and the other is the miraculous way." "What do you
mean by that?" "The natural way is that God will help

us out of this mess. The miraculous way would be to try
to do it by ourselves." The rabbi had it right. If the
Jews and the Arabs and the British and the French and
the Russians and the Americans would accept responsibility "to do justice, and to love kindness, and to walk
humbly" (Micah 6:8) in our national and international
affairs, God's help would be our natural ally and we
would find a way through our differences. But if we
trust to our own skill and cleverness, to intrigue and
expediency and power politics, then it really will be a
miracle if any of us come through.

And, again, what is true socially is true individually.
When we accept responsibility for religion in the home,
God somehow enables us to have the time for it; when
we accept responsibility for the common welfare, we
find that business prospers. When we accept responsibility for a cheerful and inviting home, we find that our
families would rather be there than anyplace else. When
we accept responsibility, God helps us to fulfill it.

Which brings us to this: *if we accept and discharge
one responsibility, we'll have another to perform.* That
may hardly seem fair, but that's what happened to
Jonah. After Nineveh repented and changed its ways,
God naturally enough didn't bring the destruction upon
it that Jonah had proclaimed. God, after all, was more
interested in living saints than in dead sinners! But
Jonah was hurt; the more he thought about it, the mad-
der he became. God had made a liar out of him in front
of all these pagans whom he despised anyhow! And the
fourth chapter tells how God laid on Jonah the new
responsibility of learning to forgive. His first responsibility—to proclaim destruction in the name of the Lord
—when responded to led to a new responsibility: to
learn how to forgive.

Is life therefore nothing but a dreary round of ever-increasing burdens that finally crush us? No! This fact—that responding to responsibility brings another to our door—is one of the things that makes life worth living. It makes for joy and growth. Here is a baby. It must prove responsive to a number of responsibilities. The first, I suppose, is to gasp for air when the doctor suitably stimulates it. It must cry when it's hungry. But the time comes when it must *not* cry when slapped and when it must wait patiently for dinner. At which stage is its life richer and more enjoyable? It must respond to its muscular responsibilities—to lift its head, focus its eyes, pull itself up, crawl, walk, then to run, jump, climb. Who would exchange the last responsibilities for the first?

For those inclined, nevertheless, to suspect that life is thus a rat race I must insist that it is literally this which makes it an interesting rat race! Experimenters have discovered that mice run faster in wheels that present a challenge to them—for example, a triangular or square wheel, or one that has hurdles in it they have to jump. And, what is more, if given a choice between a simple round wheel and a more difficult type, they prefer the ones that are harder! It is the fact that responding to one responsibility with God's help always brings another to our door that makes life enjoyable rather than simply endurable. As a scientist put it a while back, "There is nothing more productive of problems than a really good solution."

We can see what we have been saying in the story of a man we all admire. When he was twelve his father died, and at twenty he found himself the executor for his oldest brother's estate and he was cast, sink or swim, into the world of business, politics, and war. He retired

rather early in life from military and public affairs to
the management of his own farm, but after a couple of
years he was writing melancholy and gloomy letters to
friends: his father had died young, so had his oldest
brother; not yet forty-five, he was sure that his own life
was drawing to its close. He spoke of his "approaching
decay." Then came signs of war out of Europe, and he
was called back into military service. He responded and
did a fine job, being credited by most with the tenacity
and the headwork that won the war. He retired once
more from public life, with considerable honor, at the
age of fifty-two. Before long he was downcast again. He
wrote in one letter, "I am descending the hill . . . and
soon expect to be entombed in the mansions of my
fathers." His family and doctor worried about his melan-
cholia. Public affairs were in a turmoil. Again his fellows
called upon him for leadership, and again he responded.
For a man "descending the hill" he did a pretty good
job: the Constitutional Convention, the Presidency,
"first in war, first in peace, and first in the hearts of his
countrymen." Why? In no small measure because George
Washington was responsive to responsibility.

II

Jonah may be the most familiar but least understood
book in Scripture! It is not a study in marine biology or
botany, and it was not written to induce faith by report-
ing the miraculous. It is more nearly a cartoon for the
editorial page. It is a quick sketch using traditional materials and figurative ideas to make a point. It is an Old
Testament parable and to inquire as to whether or not
it actually happened is as pointless as inquiring whether
or not Jesus had in mind an actual event when he told

the story about the good Samaritan, or whether he could have given you the name, address, and social security number of the prodigal son!

In the specific context of its own time and place Jonah was a protest against narrow Jewish nationalism and religious bigotry. It was intended as an antidote to the vengeful and vindictive spirit which poisons such books as Obadiah and Esther, a spirit which became all too popular in the nation structured by Ezra and Nehemiah.

In the context of our own time and place it also has something to say, so let us pursue it a little farther.

It tells us to be careful lest our virtues become our vices. The attitudes among the Jews of the fourth or fifth century B.C. which Jonah excoriates were ones that had their roots in good soil. Their fierce, narrow patriotism and religious exclusivism were flowers gone to seed, so to speak. There is a kind of patriotism which is good and noble; there is a kind of religious conviction and discipline which is wholesome and admirable. But, like every virtue in the book, patriotism and religious conviction can degenerate into vices.

There is a real danger that our American virtues are thus deteriorating. It looks very much as though our great power has corrupted us. Our faith in freedom seems to have deteriorated into a fear of Communism. Our belief in majority rule may be deteriorating into the stifling of dissent. Our faith in God gives indications of becoming a heresy hunt. We need continually to be on the alert lest our virtues become vices, or as Jesus put it, lest our light become darkness (Matt. 6:23).

Then again, *this little book reveals our need to become conscious of what we are unconsciously doing.* The reason the prophet had to speak out to his people was that they were unconscious of their pride and prejudice.

Sometime ago a thoughtful Chinese remarked that during the last generation something like twenty-five thousand Chinese students came to this country. Few of them ever saw the inside of an American home. Most of them suffered indignities of one sort or another, indicating plainly enough that most Americans regard Orientals as inferiors. Many of them are now in mainland China and we are reaping as hatred and hostility what we sowed, for the most part, all unconsciously. Europe and America alike are reaping a harvest of distrust, suspicion, and unfriendliness in Africa from the seed we and our fathers sowed there.

Let me quote without comment a report once turned in by some Every Member Visitation callers after they visited in one home:

> Their eighth-grader . . . is bored in Sunday school . . . and she is worried he will not want to go anymore. She is very busy with Symphony, Junior Symphony, and . . . [another civic group], and although she feels guilty about saying no to requests from the church, she feels she doesn't have time and energy to teach Sunday school, etc., and wishes the church would stop asking her.

Well, there is little hope for a real improvement in any of our problems as individuals or as a nation until we become conscious of what we are unconsciously doing. That is true of psychoanalytic problems. It is true of the church. It is true of the adolescent out for kicks. It is true in education.

What is the answer for our condition? Let me mention some things The Book of Jonah prescribes.

Jonah insists that *it is the duty of a religious person to be loving.* He is to be universally loving, as God is.

The last chapter in the book shows Jonah sulking. He will not try to love the Ninevites, and he is angry that God should. As John put it centuries later, "He who says he is in the light and hates his brother is in the darkness still" (I John 2:9).

Here are the South African and Rhodesian whites. They are trying to live without loving, but the rest of us watch with grave apprehension. Stalin dealt with recalcitrant peasants without love, and there was no love in Hitler's answer to the "Jewish problem." There's not much of it in the KKK or in the Black Panthers. But surely living without loving has been tried thoroughly enough and long enough to demonstrate that it doesn't work! The religious person is to love as God loves, "with all his heart."

Jonah also implies that *it is the duty of a religious person to be rational*. It pictures God as reasoning with Jonah, trying to show the prophet his inconsistency in pitying the destruction of a plant but not that of a city full of human beings and animals. A religious man, it suggests, ought to be amenable to reason. God says to men, according to Isaiah (ch. 1:18), "Come now, let us reason together."

That is one of the great needs of our time. A good many of us organize our thoughts and lives and reactions in the manner of the college student described by Stephen Leacock. He asked what courses the student was taking. The boy replied that he was taking Turkish, music, and religion. Was he planning to be a "choirmaster in a Turkish cathedral?" asked Leacock. "No, no," was the impatient answer, "I'm going into insurance. But Turkish comes at nine, music at ten, and religion at eleven. So they make a good combination." Mere personal convenience, pleasure, or comfort is no rational way to decide upon a course of study. Nor are they rational ways to approach other problems.

There is a sense in which it can be said that the whole mental life is a process of rationalizing experience, arranging it in meaningful order. The consciousness of a newborn baby must be just a "blooming, buzzing, confusion," and his greatest task is to make sense out of apparently unrelated sensations. The process of doing it is what we call "learning" or "maturing." It is the extension of that kind of process which must be carried on if we are to whip the personal and social problems of our time. Until we can reduce their factors to elements that are reasonable or unreasonable to men of goodwill we will be powerless. Even love, with all its power, "going it blind," will not suffice.

There are two key words to The Gospel According to John, and, one might almost say, to the entire New Testament. One of them is *logos* which is usually translated "Word" but which often is translated "reason." And the other is *agape*—"love." Love and reason—these are humanity's best tools! Can any Christian, for example, reasonably believe that God loves a Jew more than an Arab? Or a Christian more than a Hindu? Or a white more than a black? Or an American boy more than a Viet Cong guerrilla? It is the duty of a religious person not only to be loving but also to be rational. In the postwar decade Kansas City's Negro population overflowed its earlier districts. "The pattern was familiar and explosive": panic sales by white residents, mass meetings, homemade bombs. Then a Christian stood up and in the name of love and reason denounced the blockbusting and the panic; he followed by putting a sign on the front lawn of his house: "Not For Sale—Neither My Home

Nor My Moral Convictions." The exodus slowed to a normal rate of turnover and I have heard of no further incidents in that neighborhood.

Paraphrasing Arnold Toynbee, the English historian, another has written: "Apathy can be overcome only with enthusiasm and enthusiasm can be aroused only by two things. One is the ideal that takes the imagination by storm. The other is a definite and intelligible plan for carrying the ideal into practice." [14] Let the ideal—love, undiscourageable goodwill, as universal as God's own— take our imaginations by storm, and let it be wedded in us to reason—a definite and intelligible plan—and we will find God's way through the problems of our time!

III

Jonah seems to end on an incongruous note. The words hardly seem to be very significant, but the more one thinks about them, the more they mean. In the last chapter, God is trying to reason with Jonah, trying to broaden the prophet's outlook and modify his religious and national parochialism. He gets Jonah to feeling some compassion for a plant that has died suddenly and then he pulls the rug from under him with a rhetorical question: "And the Lord said, 'You pity the plant, for which you did not labor, nor did you make it grow, which came into being in a night, and perished in a night. And should not I pity Nineveh, that great city, in which there are more than a hundred and twenty thousand persons who do not know their right hand from their left, and also much cattle?' " (Jonah 4:10–11.) Why tack on that bit about the cattle?

For one thing, that bit about the cattle indicates that *God is interested in property.* Cattle, livestock, was to the

Near East what it was to Texas before oil was found in either place—it was wealth, capital, property. It was taxable and convertible; it was a blue-chip investment in peacetime and a number-one spoil in war. And this little book whose main theme is God's interest in and concern for people is wise enough to know that such concern extends to property also. God is interested in property; as someone else has put it, to God "matter matters." He is interested particularly in what we do with it and what it does to us.

Every year there is a "Law Day, U.S.A.," and no one should understand God's concern better than lawyers. They know how important property is; they know how essential it is that property rights be respected; they know how it represents blood, sweat, and toil; they know that owners tend to take a rather direct and personal interest in property. Then again, no one should understand better than lawyers what it is that God expects of us in the use of property. They can understand that at the very least he expects us to be good tenants, and take reasonable care of what we are occupying for a while. They can understand that he would like some return on his investment. Moreover, they should be better able than most of us to know what stewardship means: they know what it is to hold something in trust for someone else; they know what it is to be a trustee; they know what it is to have the "power of attorney." And those are the ways that the Bible describes our relationship to God's property. "The earth is the Lord's and the fulness thereof" (Ps. 24:1)—we have the power of attorney over it for a little while, but we never own it and we are ultimately responsible for what we do with it. "To whom much is given, of him will much be required." (Luke 12:48.) "Also the cattle" —to God, matter matters! He is interested in it; he is interested in what it does to us; he is interested in what we do with it.

Then again, that bit about the cattle suggests that *God is interested in life.* He is interested in every living thing; he is interested even in those forms of life which we take for granted. Perhaps in no other place in the entire Bible is the love of God for all his creatures more clearly indicated. As Coleridge's "ancient mariner" put it,

> He prayeth best, who loveth best
> All things both great and small;
> For the dear God who loveth us,
> He made and loveth all.[15]

Albert Schweitzer, who couldn't drop a post into a post-hole until he had made sure that no ant or bug would be squashed in the process, was not a romantic simpleton. He knew as well as anyone that life lives on life and that to save a wound from infection the surgeon must kill millions of bacteria. By reverence for life he did not mean that we can get through life without destroying other forms of life. What he meant was that we do not have to be cruel or callous. His plea is that we be decent and responsible in our attitude toward life wherever we find it.

That bit about the cattle, furthermore, reminds us of *the mysterious benevolence of God.* As the story goes, the livestock in Nineveh never knew how close they had come to being wiped out. They never knew that God had any concern for them as life or even as property. His goodwill toward them was totally undecipherable by them.

I do not want anyone to press this too far, but I think there is something there worth remembering. There is a mysteriously benevolent quality about life; there is something that takes care of us more than we know. When we think about radiation in space and the cheerless surface of the moon we are inclined to say that the universe is a pretty hostile environment. But must we not also say that it is a very friendly environment? If it weren't, we wouldn't be here at all! If it weren't, we wouldn't find out about the dangers of radiation until too late. God takes care of us more than we know. I once heard a panel of physicians discussing mental and emotional problems. One of them pointed out that while there is not really very much known about depression, and little that can be done by way of effective treatment, it is a self-curing disease. That is, people almost invariably get over it in a year or eighteen months whether or not they have any kind of treatment! Which, of course, is only another illustration of something all physicians depend upon all the time, something we commonly call the "healing power of nature" but which Harvard's famous medical professor Richard C. Cabot called the "healing power of God."

Long before he was famous, Martin Luther King, Jr., once addressed a meeting, trying to convey a strength and courage he himself did not feel. For weeks the tension had been mounting, telephone threats against himself and his family had reached a new pitch. After the meeting, one of his parishioners, Mother Pollard, cornered him. "Something is wrong with you," she said. "You didn't talk straight tonight." He tried to deny that anything was wrong. But she wouldn't be brushed off. "You can't fool me," she said. "I know something is wrong. Is it that we ain't doing things to please you? Or is it that the white folks are bothering you?" Before he could answer, she went on, "I dun told you we is with you all the way." And then, with an even more radiant certainty, "But even if we ain't with you, God's gonna take care of you." And years later the Nobel Prize winner confessed that those words were still a source of strength and courage to him.

Well, that is the Biblical promise, not only to him but to us. "The Lord is my shepherd, I shall not want" (Ps. 23:1), wrote one psalmist. "Blessed be the Lord, who daily bears us up" (Ps. 68:19), wrote another. "Are not five sparrows sold for two pennies?" asked our Lord. "And not one of them is forgotten before God." (Luke 12:6.)

Jonah comes down to what Thomas Hardy once put in a couple of lines:

> I never cared for Life: Life cared for me,
> And hence I owed it some fidelity.[16]

And Albert Schweitzer put it even more succinctly. He was once asked by the American playwright Thornton Wilder: "Tell me, doctor, at the age you have reached" —he was then nearly eighty—"how do you feel about the loves of your youth—Bach, Wagner, Goethe, Kant, Hegel? One does change in the course of a lifetime." And the great humanitarian answered in French, *"Moi? Je suis fidel."* "Me? I am faithful." [17]

Chapter 3

THE LAW
AND THE GOSPEL

"THE LAW" is the traditional Jewish term for the first
five books of the Bible, and the contention has been that
they were all written by Moses. There is no very good
reason for believing that, but there is every reason to believe that that intrepid prophet (Deut. 34:10) was the
source for the basic ideas and convictions which have
been both law and gospel for the Jews to this very day.
Perhaps some of these are best seen in the books of
Deuteronomy and Leviticus, to which we turn now.

I

Biblical scholars are agreed that Deuteronomy is a
reflection of Moses' spirit. "Nowhere else in the Old
Testament do we breathe such an atmosphere of generous devotion to God, and of large-hearted benevolence
towards man; and nowhere else is it shown with the same
fulness of detail how these principles may be made to
permeate the entire life of the community." [18] In form
Deuteronomy is cast as though it were a sermon by Moses,
or a compilation of his last three addresses to the people

of Israel, and its central themes are a rediscovery and re-emphasis and reinterpretation of what Moses had to say.

First of all, Deuteronomy says that *religion is for all of life*. Religious principles and ideas are not simply for Sunday adornment, but for weekday use. Religion applies not only to how you say your prayers, but to what you eat and what you wear. Those old dietary and clothing laws in Deuteronomy seem pretty archaic now, but their principle is sound. Religion applies not only to your theories about God, it applies also to your economics and to the social status you accord your brother. Some of those laboring under the impression that capitalism is divinely ordained would suffer a rude awakening if they would read Deut. 15:1, where the command is that every seven years all debts are to be wiped from the slate! The laws so tediously enunciated in Deuteronomy attempt to cover every phase of life—religious, domestic, social, national. There is no distinction between the sacred and the secular—all is sacred.

The book of Deuteronomy says to us also that there is a time for intolerance. That rather jars us, I think. We have been schooled to believe that tolerance is a virtue. "Intolerant" is almost an epithet in our time. Well, tolerance *is* a cardinal virtue and in many an area we need more of it. But, like every other virtue in the book, tolerance can become a vice. There is a time for intolerance. If I were stricken with acute appendicitis, I would not want a doctor who took a fifty-fifty view of surgery. I would want one who rather intolerantly brushed aside the mouthings of so-called "religious" healers and dietary quacks to perform an appendectomy. When I go up in a plane I do not want to have a pilot who is very tolerant on the question of drinking on the job. I want one who says, intolerant as it may be, that alcohol and work do

not mix. I think that Negroes are right in their intolerance of our housing and schooling traditions. The book
of Deuteronomy is likewise intolerant of false, immoral,
and unethical religious and social practices. It proclaims
God as jealous of his place. It categorically forbids the
worship of idols. "Justice, and only justice" is its command in social relations. If there is a bad apple found in
the barrel, it is to be cast out. The divine hostility to evil
is absolute. There is a time for intolerance. It does not
bless all intolerance, but it commends that required by
justice.

There is something intolerant and uncompromising
about truth and justice and love. The word "moderation"
occurs just once in the Bible, and there it is a mistransla-
tion (Phil. 4:5)! Moses was almost uncontrollably intolerant of the unjust slavery of his people. Martin
Luther confessed that when he was angry he prayed and
preached well. William Ellery Channing, the influential
American preacher, used to say: "Ordinarily I weigh one
hundred and twenty pounds; when I'm mad I weigh a
ton." The Gospel According to Mark tells us that when
Jesus saw a deed of mercy being hindered by a ceremonial
triviality he "looked around at them with anger" (Mark
3:5). When the disciples tried to brush off the little children who were clamoring to see him, Jesus was indignant
(Mark 10:14).

One of the voices that stirred the conscience of this
nation to the monstrous injustice of slavery was William
Lloyd Garrison. He was, of course, accused of intolerance
and ungentlemanly immoderation. He replied: "On this
subject I do not wish to think or speak with moderation.
No! Tell a man whose house is on fire to give a moderate
alarm; tell him moderately to rescue his wife from the
hands of a ravisher; tell the mother to gradually extricate

her babe from the fire into which it has fallen—but urge me not to use moderation in a cause like the present."

If the strictures against heathen practices and the punishments prescribed for those who fail to keep the law in Deuteronomy seem harsh and lacking in a desirable universalism, remember the time from which they came and appreciate the fact that there is a time for intolerance.

Once more, *Deuteronomy makes it plain that there is only one real choice in life: the choice between obedience and disobedience.* That is the extent of our freedom; we can obey God or we can disobey him. There is no middle ground. "I set before you this day a blessing and a curse" (Deut. 11:26), he says. And again: "I have set before you this day life and good, death and evil. If you obey . . . , you shall live. . . . But if your heart turns away, . . . you shall perish" (Deut. 30:15 ff.). Ultimately the only real choice we have is between obedience and disobedience.

I am fully aware that the accent on obedience is not very popular these days. The marriage service used to include a vow for the woman to "love, honor, and obey" her husband. It was taken out in a move toward abolishing the double standard; and surely a marriage ceremony ought not to imply that one partner is inferior to the other! I would not put it back in. But let us not think that we can take obedience out of married life! Unless each partner is obedient to the needs of the other, and unless both "steadfastly endeavor to do the will" of their heavenly Father, there will be no lasting happiness. A child who has never been taught to be obedient to his parents is a child deformed. A student who has not learned obedience to academic disciplines will not make much of a mark. The workman who is disobedient to the requirements of his job will never be a craftsman. The only real choice we have in life is obedience or disobedience to the Highest.

Deuteronomy, furthermore, reveals that love of God is the key to human relations. Love to God, as the motive of human action, is its characteristic doctrine. It holds that men who do not love God will not love one another. I do not think, for example, that anyone can give Karl Marx a fair reading and not be convinced that he was terribly in earnest in his effort to find a key to the correction of the gross economic and social injustice of nineteenth-century Europe. Communist theory in some ways is very noble and has attracted many socially concerned people by its very idealism. Unfortunately, as operational Communism has plainly shown, social and economic and cultural revolution do not necessarily produce the justice and brotherhood which Marx thought they would. Communist theory fails at the point of its motivation. It has no motive great enough to save men from exploiting one another in a struggle for power.

Deuteronomy is right: those who do not love God will not long love their fellows. Out of his World War II imprisonment by the Japanese, Langdon Gilkey wrote a book called *Shantung Compound.* Gilkey is the son of missionaries to China and he says that the Weihsien camp, where he was held, was relatively civilized. There was no overt torture, but there was never enough food and no such thing as privacy. Before long, he noticed, even the missionaries were squabbling with their fellow prisoners and stealing—if the occasion offered itself—from the communal supplies. The fabric of their life became so rotten that it almost threatened their very existence as a community. The only man who could be trusted to guard supplies without stealing any for him-

self was an alcoholic, and many of those who stole looked
down their moral noses at him for drinking! But there
were a few genuine saints; and looking back, Gilkey can
see now that it was only those with a living and active
faith in a transcendent Creator who were free enough to
respond to the challenges of prison life nobly rather than
collapse under them as a threat. Loyalties to mundane
concerns are a perpetual source of social antagonisms;
only when one is faithful to a Being beyond the earthly
is he free enough to love and live for his fellows.

The original machine for driving piles for building
foundations used a heavy weight which was lifted up and
then made to fall upon the head of the pile. Its force
came from its elevation. So with us, who in the spirit of
Deuteronomy would reform all that which is less than
Christian and come down with pile-driver blows upon
contemporary injustice and inhumanity. All our power
will depend upon the elevation of our spirits in the love
of God!

II

The book of Leviticus is probably "the least read book
in the Old Testament." In my judgment the reason is
that it is the dullest book in the Bible. It has virtually
no narrative; "it contains a maximum of precept and a
minimum of action." It deals for the most part with matters that have long since been dead letters for the Jews, to
say nothing of Christians. It has none of the poetry of
the Psalms, none of the personalities of the Gospels, none
of the thunder and lightning of the Revelation. It is
pretty dull stuff.

The chief reason, I would say, for the average Christian
to read and make every effort to understand Leviticus is

that a knowledge of it helps him to understand the thought patterns and word usages of the New Testament. It describes religious observances and the Temple ritual "that lasted until after the time of Jesus." In its light, references that are otherwise obscure—such as the splitting of the curtain of the Temple in two—become intelligible. With it for a background such a book as The Letter to the Hebrews loses much of its strangeness. It is true that one may be a Christian without having an intimate knowledge of the sacrificial system it describes, but it does not follow that one can safely and surely understand the New Testament without some understanding of Leviticus.

In addition to its historical value, however, Leviticus has some things to say about religion and life which in themselves are worthy of our consideration.

For one thing, Leviticus reminds us that *we need some negatives.* It has an abundance of specific prohibitions and taboos, "thou shalt nots." "You shall not steal," "You shall not oppress your neighbor," "You shall not go up and down as a slanderer among your people," "You shall not hate your brother in your heart." (Lev. 19:11–17.)

Negatives have always been unpopular, of course. Nobody likes to be forbidden anything. And in these days of "positive thinking" they have fallen into particular disrepute. Almost all of us have been taught that one of the great distinctions between the Old and the New Testament is that for the most part the one is negative and the other positive. Psychology has shown the limited utility of prohibitions in motivating behavior. Every parent knows that almost the surest way to get a child to do something is to tell him not to!

And yet, we need some negatives. The New Testament

has its great affirmations, but in the three chapters of the Sermon on the Mount it has no less than fifteen "don'ts" also! Social life is not possible without restraints. Lay it to what cause you will, we have not yet proved capable of driving our automobiles with such maturity that we always think of the other driver first, never take a chance, never lose our patience, always yield the right-of-way— always doing the things we ought to do and never doing the things we ought not to do! We need the negatives of stop signs and policemen!

Leviticus also asserts that *worship is not an adornment of life, but a necessity.* It is not an elective in the University of Life, but part of the core curriculum. It was not a preacher, but a physicist at one of our state universities who said that he had come to three conclusions. "The first is that salvation is not to be found in science. Secondly, we must have a moral revival. Thirdly, we can have no moral revival without a living religion." To which the book of Leviticus reminds us to add: "Fourthly, we can have no living religion without worship." Worship, it declares, is to be woven into every part of the fabric of life. Within its concern are agriculture, public health, sanitation, social customs, individual failures and guilt, religious observances, national policy, moral regulation, family life, and practically anything else you'd care to mention!

Why does it put such a premium upon worship? And why ought we to do the same? Simply because great living is not possible without worship. Through the years it has been amply demonstrated that worship does something for us which nothing else does. One need not elaborate on the theme that most of us find it easy to forget our own shortcomings, nor that—paradoxically—

we universally are repelled by those who forget their own shortcomings and suffer from "pressure of the halo." What is it that does as much to remind us that we are sinners and to knock us off our pedestals of self-regard as worship? Bishop Ensley once observed that during his student days in Germany there was a national holiday which had been inaugurated after World War I. It was called *Busstag,* and was a day of national penitence. The people went into their churches to confess and mourn their national sins. But when Hitler came to power, one of his first moves was to abolish *Busstag.* "He thought it was unbecoming to a people to acknowledge that it had sinned." And, says the Bishop, "the decline of Germany morally proceeded unabated from that hour."

All of us know, conversely, that there are deep within us moods of penitence and dedication which, when kindled, bring us to our finest hours. Is there anything which touches them as often as worship does? Historian Winston Churchill quotes with approbation Burke's words: "The means by which Providence raises a nation to greatness are the virtues infused into great men." Can you name a way more virtues have been infused than through worship? Someone has likened living today to turning on a radio full blast and then spinning the dial —a jumble of sounds and voices from which one can hardly make sense. Is there anything in the world that can match worship for giving us the quiet, reflective, steady perspective? Worship is not an adornment of life, but a necessity.

Leviticus tells us, furthermore, that *holiness is the way to happiness.* One of the major sections of the book is often called the "holiness code" because of its recurring refrain, "You shall be holy; for I the Lord your God am

holy." And it is from this section that Jesus quoted the
commandment he rated second of all and like unto the
first and greatest: "You shall love your neighbor as yourself."

Scriptural holiness is a compound of several ingredi-
ents. It is an attitude not only of love but also of awe and
respect toward God, a personal feeling of acceptance by
God, a way of personal and social conduct approved by
God. It is a negative reaction to filth, disease, corruption;
it is a positive pull toward purity, cleanliness, health.

No one, of course, is against purity, cleanliness, health.
But many of us are overlooking the only root from which
such flowers actually grow: an overwhelming sense of the
holiness of God. The old Hebrew idea was that the
presence of God was so awesome that it would kill a man
who was not properly prepared to approach him. The
idea currently fashionable in many circles seems to be
that God is so companionable and indulgent that he may
be approached at any time, in any spirit or posture, and
with the most informal familiarity. Be it said to the
credit of Leviticus that it never forgets that God is *God*
—our Father, yes, but One whom the New Testament
also describes as "a consuming fire" and of whom it says,
"It is a fearful thing to fall into the hands of the living
God." In Leviticus "there is a unique sense of the
majesty and presence of God," expressed by the recurring,
"I am the Lord." And in the code of holiness we hear,
as it were, "the solemn strokes of a great . . . bell, proclaiming the dwelling of the Most High God amongst
men, and calling them to worship and obey." Never forget that it was not a sentimental humanism that em-
powered Gandhi or drove Albert Schweitzer on in Africa!
It was an idea about God and his demands upon men!

A part of the good news of the Bible is that such holiness leads to happiness. That it is, in fact, the only way to enduring happiness. Once I was being quizzed by some fraternity boys about my religious beliefs. I implied that I thought there are probably chances for moral and spiritual growth after death as well as before. So one of them wanted to know: "Why bother with this religious stuff now? If one still has a chance to repent and be saved later, why not eat, drink, and be merry?" The answer is obvious. He is assuming that the religious life is something grim and formidable; no joy, only iron discipline and self-denial. I believe the opposite: the religious life is the good life, the happy life, the rich and rewarding life, and he who avoids it cheats himself. Holiness is the way to happiness.

"I wish I had your creed," someone is reported to have remarked to Pascal, "then I would live your life." And swift as a rapier came the reply, "Live my life and you will have my creed." Doing and knowing are blood relatives. So the book of Leviticus—with its negatives, its ritual, its worship, its holiness—really is one more Biblical witness that "obedience is the organ of spiritual knowledge." And so with Christianity. As the gospel of Jesus Christ, who knew and studied Leviticus and then went far beyond it, put it, "If any man's will is to do . . . [God's] will, he shall know whether the teaching is from God" (John 7:17).

Psychoanalyst Bruno Bettelheim is a recognized authority on children's emotional development. He has made some interesting and seemingly paradoxical remarks about youthful protesters:

> When I see some of these students—"unwashed" and "unkempt"—I cannot help thinking: "There goes another youngster who, as an infant, was prac-

tically scrubbed out of existence by his parents in the name of good hygiene and loving care." [19]

Which most of us would regard, I suppose, as a warning against being too strict and rigid. But, on the other hand, he also said:

The political content of student revolt is most of all a desperate wish that the parent should have been strong in the convictions that motivate his actions. This is why so many of our radical students embrace Maoism, why they chant "Ho Ho Ho Chi Minh" in their demonstrations. They chant of strong fathers with strong convictions.[20]

Which is to say that their parents were not strict and rigid enough!

These, of course, are not absolute contradictions. Every sensitive parent knows how fine the line is between being too permissive and not being permissive enough, and every parent knows that he errs sometimes on one side and sometimes on the other. The nub of what he is saying seems to me to be that *human lives need some rails to run on;* we need guidelines and checkpoints built into us, or laid down for us, or learned by us, from our parents and social institutions. We never attain maximum happiness or effectiveness by simply expressing every urge or impulse that we feel. Too much repression leads to disaster; so does too little; and an inconsistent swinging from one extreme to the other is probably worst of all. The problem, not merely for parents, but for us all, is how to be disciplined persons without being rigid persons.

Negatives like those in Leviticus can be rails to run on. Leviticus is full of prohibitions and taboos: "You shall not steal" (ch. 19:11); "You shall not oppress your neighbor" (v. 13); "You shall not go up and down as a slanderer among your people" (v. 16); "You shall not hate your brother in your heart" (v. 17).

A year or two ago, when an attempt was being made to introduce professional soccer into this country, a well-informed Britisher was hired to do television commentary. He called the plays as he saw them—and some of them, of course, were bad. He never hesitated; he would say that so-and-so made a mistake, or a bad play. So the television executives called him in. They explained that this was negative sportscasting. He replied that he was only telling the truth. With their magnificent Madison Avenue-style wisdom they tried firmly to explain that there were two kinds of truth—the negative and the positive; on any given play he should not say that one player made a bad play, but that another made a good play. But he pointed out that often one player hadn't made a good play—he'd made only an ordinary play, or perhaps no real play at all; the other had made a *bad* play. So they let him go.

There is a quaint passage, which they say is from the Rule of St. Benedict, which goes like this:

> If any pilgrim monk come from distant parts . . . to dwell within the monastery, and will be content with the customs which he finds in the place . . . he shall be received, for as long a time as he desires. If, indeed, he find fault with anything, or expose it reasonably, and with the humility of charity, the Abbott shall discuss it prudently, lest perchance God has sent him for this very thing. But, if he have been found gossipy and contumacious in the time of his sojourn as guest, not only ought he not to be joined to the body of the monastery, but also it

shall be said to him, honestly, that he must de-
part. If he does not go, let two stout monks, in the
name of God, explain the matter to him.[21]

Even monks need some negatives!

In an effort to determine what has made some of our
secondary schools outstanding in their production of
finalists for the National Merit Scholarships, one educator quizzed the principals of thirty-eight of them—
public and private and ranging from four hundred to five
thousand pupils. Only one principal bothered to mention his physical plant as a major asset, "but their com-
ments spoke volumes: 'I am never happy except with
superior work.' 'We simply refuse to accept mediocrity.'
. . . 'When in doubt, give the lower grade.' " The power
of negative thinking!

We need some negatives. They may often be the only
adequate preparation for the positive. They can be a rail
to run on, or, to change the figure slightly, a guardrail
which keeps us on the way that leads to life.

Leviticus teaches us that *ritual can also be a rail to
run on.* Much of the book is a detailed manual for the
guidance of Israel's priests in the performance of their
duties. In one particular rite, for example, it specifies
that "the priest shall take some of the blood of the guilt
offering, and the priest shall put it on the tip of the
right ear of him who is to be cleansed, and on the thumb
of his right hand, and on the great toe of his right foot"
(Lev. 14:14). It sounds neither very attractive nor particularly helpful! Yet we would be foolish to lose sight
of something that ritual accomplished. That particular
instruction was for the purifying of a person who had
been cured of a skin disease. The Hebrews early learned
that those with infectious skin diseases must be separated

from and isolated from their fellows. In a time when disease was believed to be the direct result of sin, and sin was regarded as the only cause of disease, to be afflicted meant not only physical discomfort and quarantine but moral ostracism and a deep sense of personal failure and guilt. When the disease was gone a ritual was provided for the reinstatement of the person into the community. It was a permit from the health officer to go back to school. But it was also more than that. It was a way of relieving the person of the burden of personal guilt and getting rid of it forever. The ritual thus contributed to the well-being of all.

People thinking nostalgically about the "old-time religion" sometimes complain that we have "too much ritual" in church these days. But the truth is really that we merely have different rituals: it is just as ritualistic to wear a cutaway coat in the pulpit as a robe; it is just as ritualistic to read a responsive reading as a litany, or to announce the hymn number and the first line of a hymn as it is to print it in a bulletin; it is just as ritualistic to end a pastoral prayer with the words "as Jesus taught us to pray" and then go into the Lord's Prayer as it is to say, "Amen," pause, and then begin the Lord's Prayer. Rituals are habitual ways of doing things, that's all; and the only valid question is whether they are good ways or poor ways at the moment.

Chapter 4

THE VOICE
OF EXPERIENCE

ONE OF THE GREAT THINGS about the psalms is that they speak with the voice of experience. There is nothing theoretical or hypothetical about them. They know all our human joys and sorrows, all our hopes and anxieties, because they are the deposit of actual human situations. They reflect our ambiguities and compromises as well as our faith and our ideals. They know that "the pursuit of happiness" is always high on the human agenda. The very first psalm (in point of arrangement, not in point of time) is a sort of preface to the whole collection. What does it indicate about finding direction and purpose and happiness?

I

It calls our attention, for one thing, to *the help that books can give*. The good man is the happy man for the psalmists, the man who delights in the law—the *torah*— of the Lord. What they mean by that is what we call the first five books of the Bible, some of which we have looked at. In a broad, but not improper sense in this latter day, I think it can be said that the psalmists commend the reading of available history and biography and nonfiction and social ethics as well as religion!

The possibilities in reading need some emphasis because it is not always held in high regard. A while back I saw a sheet with recommendations for television programs. For Tuesday it recommended a mystery and suspense thriller. For Wednesday it extolled an underwater show. Friday, Saturday, and Sunday offered several choices. But for Thursday it said, "Read a book." Which was its way of saying something about television programming; but it also said something about our general attitude toward reading—something to do as a last resort!

In that kind of setting it seems to me appropriate to paraphrase Sir Arthur Conan Doyle's words and say that it is a great thing to have even a small number of really good books which are your very own. If one is really interested in the pursuit of happiness, he cannot start too soon to build his own library of solid reference books which will be the tools of his mind for a lifetime. On a deeper level one needs books that are his very own in the sense that he has read, studied, mastered, and come to love them. And on a deeper level still, the really good books that are your very own are the books that have mastered you, that say something to you, that nurture your spirit, that give you strength and inspiration for living. These books are relatively few and far between; with very few exceptions they cannot be named in advance. As a photographer may take scores of shots to get one or two good pictures, so the reader must go through a lot to have a little. Looking back over my own reading, I would say that I'm lucky to find one such book a year. But once you have found it, it never lets you go! Walt

Whitman once put it this way: "I was simmering, simmering, simmering. Emerson brought me to a boil." On one of the occasions that the apostle Paul was an enforced guest of the civil authorities he wrote to a friend asking him to bring to him a coat he had left behind and *also his books.* He knew there was nothing like them to help him find and keep a firm grip on his sense of direction.

Then again, we are more likely to keep our sense of direction if we *discipline our use of time.* A friend of mine accompanied some leading high school graduates to a university for personal interviews. The registrar inquired into how they had spent their out-of-school time and when they had told him he candidly said that he asked the question because he had discovered that the main difference between those who would go on to graduate successfully in their chosen field and those who would be dropping out along the way would be determined by how they used about an hour and a half of their free time every day. If they used it watching television, taking in every show that came to town, leading every fraternity or sorority stunt, and so on, the university could not afford to let them enroll; it needed the space for those who could discipline the use of their time.

That is true not only for students. One of the most amazingly forceful movements of the eighteenth century was the Wesleyan revival of the religious life of England which had far-reaching sociological and political effects. How could two men—John and Charles Wesley—so affect the life of their own nation and of a great land overseas? There were plenty of contributing factors, of course, but surely not least among them was the amazing way they disciplined their use of time! John's carriage was once delayed; he had already put away his papers and left his rooms. While waiting at the door, he was overheard to mutter to himself, "I have lost ten minutes forever!" Years later, when he came to write the classic instructions still given to beginning Methodist preachers, he wrote: "Be diligent. Never be unemployed. Never be triflingly employed. Never trifle away time; neither spend any more time at any one place than is strictly necessary." He was speaking from personal experience and practice, and betraying the secret of much of his own genius.

The wonderful thing about disciplining our use of time is that it enables us to have more and not less time to do with as we please. A great many people don't have much time for themselves, as the saying goes, because they never sharpen their time schedule to the place where it cuts effectively. They go around in circles, always driven by things that must be done at once because they have been put off for so long; they dribble time away in trivialities and live from crisis to crisis. "Those who work much," Thoreau once noted, "do not work hard." That is, those who get the most done are those who work for the most part unruffled by haste and refreshed by genuinely re-creative leisure. By eliminating nonessentials, they have expanded the time for real essentials. And not the least of their rewards is usually a confident sense of where they are going.

Our pursuit of happiness has more chance of success, also, when we *respond to the moral dimension of life,* when we live with moral sensitivity, when we hold a conviction that moral choices matter. That is what Psalm One is really all about, the two ways of life: the way of the righteous and the way of the wicked.

Because this sounds like pretty routine stuff, I want to call on a witness whom no one will think of as

stuffy or pious or puritanical or out of date. He was one
of our most popular and widely quoted literary figures
and a very sophisticated entertainer. His name was Ogden
Nash. After his daughter Isabel graduated from school
she spent a year abroad, and in the process met an older
man who paid her a great deal of flattering attention.
He talked at length with her in what she thought were
the most fascinating and sophisticated terms. One day
he confided that he was planning to get a divorce from
his wife. It was an old, old line. But it was all very
romantic and Miss Nash was ecstatically sure that she
was in love with him and he with her. She wrote home,
while still more or less in the clouds. But after thinking it over for a while, she came to a more realistic conclusion and sent a more sensible letter, and her famous
father answered:

Dear Isabel,
    I gather that by now you have decided that Mr.
X is too old for you, as well as being a very silly
man, but I am not pleased by the episode, and I
trust that by now you aren't either. . . .
    You should be intelligent enough to know that in
various eras of history it has been fashionable to
laugh at morals, but the fact of the matter is that
Old Man Morals just keeps rolling along and the
laughers end up as driftwood on a sand bar. You
can't beat the game, because morals as we know
them represent the sum of the experience of the
race. That is why it distressed me to find you glibly
tossing off references to divorce. You surely have
seen enough of its effects on your friends to know
that it is a tragic thing even when forced on one
partner by the vices of the other.
    Read the marriage vows again—they are not

just words, not even just a poetic promise to God.
They are a practical promise to yourself to be
happy. This I know from simply looking around
me.

It bothers me to think that you may have sloppy
—not sophisticated but sloppy—ideas about life. I
have never tried to blind you to any side of life,
through any form of censorship, trusting in your
own intelligence to learn of, and to recognize, evil
without approving or participating in it. . . .

Keep on having your gay time, but just keep
yourself in hand, and remember that generally
speaking it's better to call older men Mister.

> I love you tremendously,
> Daddy.[22]

For all his characteristically light touch, he has his
finger on something important. Those who are prone
to laugh at the moral imperative "end up as driftwood
on a sand bar." "For the Lord knows the way of the
righteous, but the way of the wicked will perish."
(Ps. 1:6.)

They say that a famous and beloved teacher of law
always opened his beginning class by putting the figures
"4" and "2" on the blackboard. Then he would ask the
class, "What's the solution?" Somebody, of course, would
answer "6." Another would hazard, "2." There being
no response from him, someone else would say, "8."
When at last no one had any more ideas he would draw
his moral: "All of you failed to ask the key question:
What is the problem? Gentlemen, unless you know what
the problem is, you cannot possibly find the answer."
So with the pursuit of happiness! This psalmist may be
a long way from the full and complete spiritual maturity
of Jesus Christ our Lord, but he at least knows what
the problem is! And by reading, disciplining our time,

and being morally sensitive with him, we may also avoid the pursuit of unhappiness.

II

There is a crooked headland jutting out from the State of Washington into the Pacific Ocean just north of the mouth of the Columbia River named Cape Disappointment. It was named that by early explorers who had entered the little bay it shelters in the hope that it was the mouth of a freshwater river. Although they were practically at the mouth of the Columbia, fog delayed them and prevented their exploring the coastline farther, and they put out to sea, marking the spot "Cape Disappointment" in a graphic expression of their feelings.

Most of us have our own private Cape Disappointments—plans that go awry, children who turn out differently than we had hoped, recognition that we feel we have earned denied us, opportunities for advancement that go to someone else. And there are many who could mark the map of their life with more than one Cape Disappointment.

There is a great line for us at such times in Psalm Forty-six. "God is our refuge and strength, a very present help in trouble." (Ps. 46:1.) This psalm has been called "the most magnificent song of faith that has ever been sung" and provided the inspiration in a dark hour for Martin Luther to write the most famous hymn of the Reformation, "A Mighty Fortress Is Our God." And its dominant theme is confidence in God's presence in the midst of trouble, disappointment, hope deferred. Let's look at some of the evidences that support such a conviction.

There is reason to believe that God visits our Cape

Disappointments with us because *there is always present a Force that makes for healing.* Let a forest fire scorch the mountains and the embers are hardly cool before a carpet of grass and wild flowers begins to cover the nakedness of the earth. Cut your finger and at once a force is at work to heal it. Even in mental and emotional breakdowns some sort of automatic, self-corrective process goes to work.

The human body displays at least four remarkable examples of this force for healing. For one thing, it has its own reserve. We have vastly more lung tissue than we actually need, for example. Dr. Trudeau worked hard for forty years, though only part of one lung was healthy. Take away 40 percent of such an organ as the liver and the remaining 60 percent will be fully adequate for normal life. Furthermore, the body maintains a delicate balance. A temperature balance that never varies more than a few degrees; a moisture balance that regulates the amount of fluid coming in and going out so that the proper proportion is always maintained; and, most delicate of all, a chemical balance constant within a few parts in a thousand. Once more, the body has a marvelous power of compensation. If a limb or a faculty or an organ is damaged beyond repair, some other part may be increased to compensate for it. The heart will enlarge two or three times if it has to. One kidney will do the work of two if it has to. Red corpuscles are made in vastly larger quantities by persons who live at high altitudes, because the air is thinner and more are needed. And finally, the body has its own lines of defense in depth. Pain is one defense; fever is another; antibodies in the blood another.

One of the classic examples of this force making for health is the case of a man in his sixties who was killed in an auto accident. His wife testified that he had always been active and vigorous and had never been sick a day in his life. Yet the autopsy showed that he had had no less than four fatal diseases—tuberculosis, cirrhosis of the liver, chronic kidney disease, and hardening of the arteries! Yet his body had defeated or quarantined them all.

This force which makes for healing is at work in social life also. Crazes for swallowing goldfish or squealing at the voice of some rock and roller sweep sections of the population from time to time. But they don't last. Demand tends to balance supply in economic relationships. The ravages of flood or earthquake or war are soon repaired when one thinks of the immensity of the damage.

A. J. Cronin once told of visiting after the war an Italian village that he had known in earlier and happier days. Now the town was bomb-gutted, bled of its youth and its future. And the few remaining townspeople mysteriously disappeared every afternoon. Yet when he followed one of them he discovered that they were working together in building a new stone church. "These people," he remarks, "who had barely a roof above their heads, upon whom lay the blight of overwhelming destruction, these women, children, and old men whom I had seen as merely beaten and extinguished shadows, had chosen, as their first united act, to construct, solely by their own effort, a new church. Not a makeshift chapel, but a finer, larger place of worship than ever they had had before."

This healing force is at work on other levels too. If we could autopsy the soul, or if we could see the rebuilding of damaged personalities, we would find it. That is why most people regain their posture after the most smashing of sorrows and disappointments.

Another thing that reminds us of the divine presence even in our disappointments is the fact that others have found him there. This is the testimony of the centuries speaking to the hours. The Hebrew words that yield the rendering, "God . . . is a very present help in trouble" may also be translated, "God is a *well-proved* help in trouble."

The essence of the scientific method is to observe certain phenomena, make a theory or model to explain these, and then to test the theory by further experience. It is a systematic form of trial and error. Which is exactly what humanity has done for thousands of years in the religious realm. And the well-proved fact is that God is a present help in trouble. Not even a sparrow "is forgotten before God," says the Master. And his word is confirmed by Anne Frank, the little Jewish girl who while in hiding from the Nazis kept such a remarkable diary. "God has not left me alone and will not leave me alone," she wrote.

Francis Thompson failed to pass his examinations as a medical student. He failed likewise in a number of other attempts to earn a living. Finally he determined to try writing, and went to London, where he was utterly unknown and lived in abject poverty. Even writing materials were beyond his means. He used some old account books someone gave him for paper. In his loneliness and defeat and disappointment he sought relief by taking laudanum—an alcoholic tincture of opium. So a man with the sensitivities of an artist and the brain of a scholar became a drug addict. But he found that God had not deserted him. In his most famous poem, "The Hound of Heaven," he retells the experience that led to his cure—the experience of God's relentless love following him insistently until he yielded to it:

I fled Him, down the nights and down the days;
   I fled Him down the arches of the years;
I fled Him down the labyrinthine ways
   Of my own mind; and in the mist of tears
I hid from Him, and under running laughter.
        Up vistaed hopes I sped;
        And shot, precipitated,
   Adown titanic glooms of chasmèd fears,
From those strong Feet that followed, followed after.
       But with unhurrying chase
       And unperturbèd pace,
   Deliberate speed, majestic instancy,
       They beat—and a Voice beat
       More instant than the Feet—
"All things betray thee, who betrayest Me." [23]

George A. Gordon tells in his autobiography of a family in New England. They had a horribly deformed son of twenty-five years or so. "To a stranger the sight of this boy or young man was painful in the extreme; it was, indeed, at first revolting." The young man was not an idiot; he was in no way deficient in intelligence, although in every member of his body he was utterly without human shape; he was unable to speak except in a series of cries which his parents and friends had learned to understand. "Only two redeeming things there were in this poor creature, his amazingly bright intelligence . . . and his capacity . . . for love. His father had been a drunkard until this child was born to him, and a spendthrift. The sight of this child, as he grew, his craving for love, his infinitely tender response to love, his intelligence and character and helplessness so wrought upon the father as completely to revolutionize his life." He became a new man. And one day he said to the young minister: "Here is God's best gift to me. Through this child God has changed my whole life from selfishness to love. In him, so unsightly to others, I see nothing but the beauty of the Lord our God."

Still another indication of God's presence in the midst of our trouble and disappointment is that at such times *unexpected powers are released, not only in ourselves, but in others also.*

I once knew a woman of firm disposition and positive temperament who was altogether conventional and orthodox. Like so many of us of the middle class the sins that so easily beset her were those of the Pharisee—the subtle spiritual pride, the quiet "holier than thou" toward those of another political or denominational affiliation. She was a good woman in the worst way, if you know what I mean.

This woman had a brother who was a sort of rolling stone. Where she was thrifty, he was inclined to buy what he wanted when he wanted it. Their political views differed about as sharply as is possible. Where the church meant a great deal to her, he was not only skeptical but scornful. Her ideals and ethics were on the puritanical side; his were of the libertine variety. As one would expect, in their mature lives their courses had separated and it is almost the exact literal truth to say that neither had ever driven the twenty-five miles or so necessary to visit the other.

When the brother was suddenly killed in an accident I expected that her reaction would be: "Well, he chose his own life and it has come to this. I am not surprised." Of course she would go through the form of sending flowers or something, but nothing more.

How wrong I was! In the hour of bereavement for that family she was a virtual tower of spiritual strength.

No member of it was more considerate, tolerant, thought-ful, humble, generous in spirit. Some totally unexpected resources were released in her.

A pearl diver once told of a thrilling and near-fatal fight he had had with a giant octopus. Giving the emergency signal to his helpers above, he tried to fight the dweller of the deep with his hand knife. But its tentacles encircled him. Three men strained above to pull him up, but they could not budge him from that fatal grip, nor the octopus from its rock foothold. Then one of them, as the boat dipped into a trough, threw the lines about a stanchion and when the next swell lifted the boat their companion was pulled relentlessly up, octopus and all, where the latter's tentacles could be severed. The lifting power of the sea had saved him. That is a parable of human life and the unexpected powers from the universe itself which surround it!

Charles Francis Potter tells in his autobiography that he once moved into a rather snobbish neighborhood where his children weren't accepted very well. So they formed a backyard club of their own and invited some kids from the wrong side of the tracks to play with them. They were soon having so much fun that the neighbor-ing kids were asking to be allowed into the club. He saw his son Myron look over one of them rather deliberately and then say: "No, go on home. Nobody can belong to this club unless he has patches on his pants." It may be that way with maturity! No one can belong who doesn't have a few patches of disappointment on his pants. God, they say, does not look us over for medals, but for scars. Even in our bitterest disappointments he is present if we but have the wit and the grace to look for him!

III

One year, as the Canadian Open Golf Tournament was nearing the close of its fourth round, Art Wall came to the eighteenth green leading Billy Casper by two strokes. Both were on in regulation figures, but Art was farthest from the hole and putted first. He went past the hole about five feet. Then it was Casper's turn—he put a 10-footer in for a birdie; Art missed his coming back, so the two ended in a tie which they played off the next day, with Casper winning.

The thing that stuck in my mind on that crucial putt of Casper's was that when it went in he momentarily fell to his knees in an attitude of thankful prayer. I doubt if he was praying, and he may not have meant anything at all by it. On the other hand, he had been converted to a rather strict and dogmatic religious persuasion a year or two before and has subsequently given his faith credit for filling a void in his life. So the question might be put, Did prayer help Billy Casper win the Canadian Open Golf Championship?

I do not know that the question can be answered by anyone other than Billy Casper, and I certainly do not intend to try. I use the incident simply to bring to your mind some of the perennial questions most of us have about prayer: Does it work? Are prayers really answered? Will God do something for us if we pray that he won't do otherwise? I have no ready-made answers. What I propose, rather, is that we hear the voice of experience speaking to us through the man who wrote the Thirty-fourth Psalm. As far as prayer is concerned, he puts his whole autobiography in one sentence: "I sought the

Lord, and he answered me, and delivered me from all my fears."

That word suggests that *prayer begins on the level of desire*. "I *sought* the Lord"—I looked for him, hunted for him, wanted to find him. To live means to want; everyone wants something—peace of mind, security, money, success, children of whom to be proud.

The first cry you and I uttered after we arrived in this world was not one of thanksgiving for our safe arrival, nor one of praise and adoration for the Creator, nor one of confession of sins. "Our first cry was of want. Religiously, too, we begin at the level of desire."

Since prayer begins with wanting, and everyone wants something, the whole subject of prayer has sometimes been presented as a way to get what one wants. This notion is prominent in much of the popular religious thought as retailed on records and in best-selling books and popular magazines. Unfortunately, it is also the parent of much skepticism about prayer. It is not uncommon to find persons for whom vital Christian faith is difficult if not impossible because they have failed to get the things for which they have prayed. "In the stress of some trial they have faithfully prayed, and no answer has come. Friends or relatives have died, or their own health has failed, or their way has been hedged up; and all the while Heaven has seemed as deaf to their cries—as the ear of the dead."

Perhaps the knot of our dilemma—that prayer begins with wanting, but that we plainly do not always get what we want—can be cut by drawing a distinction between what we want and what we need. My mother used to have a saying, "My wants are many but my needs are few." William J. Hutchins, father of the well-known former president and chancellor of the University of Chicago, was himself a college president in Kentucky. He used to tell a story about a backwoodsman who came to town and saw for the first time a stalk of bananas. "Want to try one?" a friend suggested. "No, I reckon not," was the answer. "I've got so many tastes now I can't satisfy that I ain't aimin' to take on any more." There is a difference between wants and needs.

The place where most of us most often miss the mark in prayer, I'd hazard, is in praying for what we want rather than for what we need. When Peter Marshall was stricken with his first heart attack, his wife says that seemingly a thousand times in the next few hours she closed her eyes and demanded: "God, make him well. God, please dissolve that blood clot!" But that was not real prayer, and she knew it. Tenseness and fear gripped her. Then, finally, she and a friend began together to ask *how* to pray for Peter, and courage and strength and peace began to possess her. You are really praying when you're looking for what you need and not merely for what you want.

We can further learn from this man's experience that prayer means not only to seek, but to *listen*. "He answered me." "Prayer," according to an early Christian, "is conversation with God." "Whether short or long, whether vocal or only mental, prayer should be like the conversation of a child with its father." A conversation has two sides; one not only talks, but one listens to the other person.

A lot of us, I suspect, have missed the mark in prayer at this point too. We say the grace at the table, or offer our prayers the last moment at night in bed, but don't ever leave time for God to answer. We turn our minds to other things or go to sleep! Anne Morrow Lindbergh has a provocative phrase in her little meditative gem *Gift from the Sea,* which goes like this: "For it is only framed in space that beauty blooms." "My life," she says, "lacks . . . beauty, because there is so little empty space. The space is scribbled on; the time has been filled. There are so few empty pages in my engagement pad, or empty hours in the day, or empty rooms in my life in which to stand alone and find myself. Too many activities, and people, and things. Too many worthy activities, valuable things, and interesting people. For it is not merely the trivial which clutters our lives but the important as well." [24] Did you ever try to read a page that had no margin? It's difficult. In a well-printed book the type doesn't use more than about two thirds of the space on the page—the printers call the rest "white space." It adds not only to the beauty but to the legibility of the page. So our lives need "to be framed in space" in which to hear God when he answers. "When you pray," says Jesus, "go into your room and shut the door" (Matt. 6:6) —not only to avoid ostentation but to frame yourself in some space and silence in which to listen.

If one does not listen for answers to his questions and his problems, he is not likely to receive them. Every counselor knows people who have gone through life as overgrown adolescents, flaunting a sort of know-it-all attitude about religion and its grappling with the deeper problems of life. They are not looking for answers and they do not get any; they are confident that they have them already! But then in some way their little world caves in—tragedy, accident, disaster, cruel unhappiness—and then, sometimes, they begin to look and to listen earnestly to the faith the church has been proclaiming. "There are some things a man never learns until he wants to learn them for himself. Nobody can tell him. . . . He can listen to his parents and his teachers and friends, and all the people that he counts on most and still not take it in until he is ready to listen. . . . How many times . . . have grown-up children who have come to some sort of grief gone to their parents and said, Why didn't you tell me, why didn't you tell me about this beforehand? And if the parent had the heart to say anything at all, he probably would say, My dear child, I did tell you, but you wouldn't listen."

He does not pray best, therefore, who speaks the most. He prays best whose whole life is most carefully tuned to the promptings of God's Spirit.

There is still more instruction for us in the *result* of the ancient psalmist's prayers: he "delivered me from all my fears." What we usually need more than anything else is not some material blessing, nor even to have our problems and difficulties magically vanish. What we usually need more than anything else is the poise and strength and courage to face the circumstances in which we find ourselves. Fear literally tends to scare the wits out of us. It paralyzes our judgment and inhibits our thought processes. Even mild anxiety, the psychologists tell us, hampers measurably our ability to think "without confusion, clearly."

A rather striking example of the sort of thing I am talking about came from a couple of Peace Corps volunteers who wrote not long ago to their home church. They were serving in Brazil. "Before closing," they said,

> you might be interested in reading some instructions we received in case of attack by a hungry python: "Remember not to run away; the python can run faster. The thing to do is to lie flat on the ground on your back with your feet together, arms

at your sides, head well down. The python will then try to push its head under you, experimenting at every possible point. *Keep calm* (this was underscored). You must let him swallow your foot. It is quite painless and it will take a long time. If you *keep calm* and still, he will go on swallowing. Wait patiently until he has swallowed up to about your knee. Then carefully take out your knife and insert it into the distended side of his mouth and with a quick rip slit him up!"

It sounds as though someone's leg is being pulled! But, whether that is true or not, it forcibly reminds us that there are times when "nothing is so much to be feared as fear," and there are probably few personal exercises that will do more to cast out fear than prayer.

In 1948 the Soviets blockaded Berlin. They intended to starve the populace into submission and drive the Western democracies from the city. When the blockade began, it seemed only a question of time until the iron ring would do its relentless work. A fear akin to panic gripped many a soul both in and out of the beleaguered city. Then an almost impossible thing began to happen. From the far corners of the world—Hawaii, Alaska, the Orient—those old reliable C-54s began to come. The now-famous airlift, which eventually was putting a plane a minute into Berlin, bringing in more supplies daily than the trains and trucks had before, began to operate. And with those planes and men came not only food and fuel, vital as they are, but also courage and hope and deliverance from the twin fears of hunger and tyranny. So many a beleaguered soul has found himself hedged in, surrounded on every side, and then has drawn reinforcements out of the unseen above! Prayer can always mean at least deliverance from fear.

"I sought the Lord"—prayer begins with our needs. "He answered me"—it moves on and up into conversation with and listening to the Most High. "And delivered me from all my fears"—it results in the poise and strength and courage (the cool, in our newest jargon) to face without flinching whatever it is that confronts us. That is not just theory; that is the voice of experience!

A man was once talking with a friend when he was successively interrupted by his children. First was a small boy wanting a nickel for an ice-cream cone. It was a petition easily answered. Then a little girl arrived in tears; her leg was hurt. "Daddy," she said, "kiss the pain away." And a remarkably instantaneous healing followed. Then a teen-ager with an algebra problem. That took more time. Last of all, the smallest of all. "Can't you see I'm busy?" he began impatiently. "What do you want?" "Oh," said the youngster clambering up onto Daddy's lap, "I don't want anything. I just want to sit on your lap." As a father is to a child, the Scriptures tell us, so is God to us. Will he not then freely give us everything we need when we ask him?

Chapter 5

THE ONLY PROBLEM
IN THE WORLD

THE EARLIEST PART of Isaiah, chs. 1 to 39, comes to us through the mind and heart of "Isaiah the son of Amoz" (ch. 1:1). It is by far the largest block of material in the book, and it is reason enough for both Christians and Jews to rank Isaiah as the greatest of all the prophets. His style is that of the very best period of classic Hebrew poetry, a style that was well suited to translation into English in the golden age of our own tongue. Some of its cadences are traditionally associated by Christians with the Christmas season: "For unto us a child is born, unto us a son is given: and the government shall be upon his shoulder: and his name shall be called Wonderful, Counselor, The mighty God, The Everlasting Father, The Prince of Peace" (ch. 9:6, KJV). And no one yet has bettered his description of the ancient and immortal hope of all good men for the day when the nations "shall beat their swords into plowshares, / and their spears into pruning hooks; / nation shall not lift up sword against nation, / neither shall they learn war any more" (ch. 2:4).

At the same time, the very greatness and popularity

of the book made it a subject of frequent annotation, expansion, and misunderstanding. Scarcely any of Isaiah's oracles have escaped annotation of some kind—in the pre-Christian centuries the Jews supplemented them with dazzlingly happy endings, and early Christians (reading in Greek translation) deduced from him some strange ideas about the birth of Jesus. Let us look for some of its highlights.

I

One highlight is this: "If you will not believe, / surely you will not be established" (Isa. 7:9)—*faith is the foundation of security*. This is a poetic line, and I remember my Old Testament professor's putting it this way: "If you will not have faith, / Surely you shall not have staith." The rhyme makes it easy to remember, and there really is such an English-Scotch word as "staith." It is a waterside embankment, a landing place, a wharf—a sure place to stand when tying up a boat. To have staith is to have a sure footing in dealing with continuously shifting circumstances.

Surely that is a word for our time! "Security" is one of our most overworked words: social security, national security, financial security. The writers and poets and playwrights seem to probe endlessly into our psychological need for security; advertisers play on our fear of losing whatever security we think we have banked in the form of status or popularity or something else. A great deal of religious thought concerns itself, on the one hand, almost exclusively with peace of mind—personal, inner security; or, on the other, with salvation to some form of eternal security. The doctors tell us that nervous tension—lack of security—is a factor contribut-

ing to ulcers and colitis and heart disease and alcoholism
and nobody knows how many other of the ills that
plague us!

The question for us all, then, is: How does one get
security? How does one find a sure place to stand on the
shores of time? Isaiah's answer is that you really get it
only through "a quiet and active confidence in the unseen but conclusive participation of God in the affairs
of men." He lived in a turbulent time both nationally
and internationally. Domestic difficulties and international intrigues were a dime a dozen; the immediate
situation was about as if Canada and Russia had attacked us. Hysteria was in the air, but Isaiah's word to
the king was: "Take heed, be quiet, do not fear, and do
not let your heart be faint because of these two smolder-
ing stumps of firebrands" (ch. 7:4). The invaders, he was
saying, were not serving God and God would take care
of their downfall.

Trustful obedience to God in personal and social
affairs: this is the only real and lasting source of security.
Without it, the mightiest of nuclear weapons is futile,
moth and rust will decay all our wealth, and all our
psychological self-adjustment will be vain. "For thus
said the Lord God, the Holy One of Israel, / 'In returning and rest you shall be saved; / in quietness and in
trust shall be your strength.' " (Ch. 30:15.)

Another highlight of Isaiah is his conviction that *no
one ever takes the future out of God's hands*. When
Isaiah's first son was born, the prophet gave him a
strange name: "A Remnant Will Return" (ch. 7:3; cf.
chs. 8:18; 10:21). It was a symbolic name that he could
use to suggest either peril or promise. At times he used
this living symbol as a warning, to be taken in the omi-
nous sense of "*only* a remnant shall return" from the

follies and disasters of Judah's international escapades—
only a small part of her people would survive a coming
national disaster. But at other times he meant the boy
to be an affirmation that "a remnant will return *to God*"
—that a small but purified group would survive the
coming disaster, returning in faithfulness to the God of
their fathers, new leaders would replace the old corrupt
ones, and Jerusalem would be known as a city of righteousness (ch. 1:26).

But whichever immediate application he gave to the
name, both rested on his conviction that the future was
in God's hands. No amount of cleverness or evasion or
military strength will save men from God's judgment;
no amount of defeat or disaster can take the faithful
from him.

Once when Jesus was commenting on the time of
troubles that he saw ahead for the world in his time he
said that these were but "the beginning of the sufferings" (Mark 13:8). The overtone of his meaning doesn't
come through the English translation very well. What
he was saying was that the terrible events were the "birth
pangs" of a better day; they were suffering for a purpose
and with a promise.

That was true not only in Isaiah's or Jesus' time; it is
true of those amazing Negroes in our time who have
conducted themselves with dignity and restraint while
their churches have been bombed, their leaders shot
from ambush, their children killed, and they themselves
attacked by police dogs, fire hoses, and all the demonic
instruments of power and fear and hatred. "There is
nothing meaningless or inglorious about that kind of
trouble." It qualifies as the beginning of sufferings, the
birth pangs of a better day. And it is motivated by the
same faith that sustained Isaiah of old: no one takes the

future out of God's hands. As a black cabdriver put it to a white passenger who was commiserating with him about a recent outrage: "Don't worry, the future belongs to us." Somehow that reminds me of Jefferson's word: "I tremble for my country when I reflect that God is just." There is both judgment and promise in Isaiah's certainty that no one takes the future out of God's hands.

This brings us to a third highlight of Isaiah, his exhibition of *the potency of religious experience.* The sixth chapter is "the most revealing page he ever wrote." It is one of the first and perhaps the greatest of all descriptions of intense, personal, spiritual experience written by the man who experienced it. It is the classic description of the "raw stuff" of religion, so to speak, as the stars are the "raw stuff" of astronomy, or plants are the "raw stuff" of botany—the primary datum to be investigated, studied, understood as best we may. The one thing we cannot do with it is dismiss it casually, because it has been the mainspring of so many notably strong and influential lives.

A preacher friend of mine, in his pastoral rounds, was calling on a man who had had a series of acute coronary attacks. He was a simple and commonsense sort of man, not given to flights of the imagination or ecstatic raptures. He told how the pain of the last attack was so great that it seemed almost to tear him apart and he found himself wishing he could lose consciousness. But just when it seemed that he couldn't stand it another moment, he felt a tap on his shoulder. He turned his head to see who was there and what the person wanted. But no one was there; the only other people in the room were another patient and a couple of visitors talking to him. Then he felt the tap again, and the thought

dawned that maybe it was God's way of trying to reach
him. "I realized," he said, "that I didn't have to stand
this all alone, and I thought that God could help me
and that if he was willing to do so, unworthy as I was,
I would be more grateful than words could tell." And
the pain started to ease. He was a lover of flowers and
he began to think that in heaven he might be allowed
to have a small plot of them to care for; and at that the
thought of dying became almost a pleasure. Then, as he
looked at the bleak hospital wall he seemed to see,
through an opening, into a flower garden that was beyond words in its beauty. He himself had grown some
lovely flowers, and had visited some of the world's great
gardens, but he had never seen anything like this.

We all know, of course, that the mind can play tricks
on us, particularly when we are receiving medication or
when we are under duress. But is there anyone who
wants to say that the man didn't see any flowers—that
the experience was meaningless? I, for one, would say
that when God reveals himself to us we can only describe
the feeling in the words that mean the most to us—
Moses and the burning bush, the boy Samuel in his
obedient wonder, Isaiah and a dramatic religious ceremony, Jesus at his baptism, Paul on the road to Damascus, Wesley's heart being strangely warmed, Handel com-
posing that matchless music which blesses both Christmas and Easter, and to many another soul in flowers or
something else. It is the most potent of human experiences.

II

Isaiah is a long and in many ways a difficult and obscure book, particularly to anyone who is not conversant

with the history and politics of the ancient Near East. No one should try to read it without having at hand a good annotated Bible, or a commentary, or a Bible dictionary. Like Caesar's Gaul, it pretty well divides itself into three parts. The first thirty-nine chapters, which we have been considering, for the most part come from the eighth century B.C., while the other two parts (chs. 40 to 55 and chs. 56 to 66) from a period several centuries or more later. Isaiah, in other words, is a good deal like the books of Psalms and Proverbs: it is a sort of anthology, or a collection of collections.

Its second and third sections are of particular interest to Christians because it was in these that Jesus found so much meaning from the outset of his ministry (Luke 4:16–20; cf. Isa. 61:1, 2) to the last week of his mortal life (Mark 11:17; cf. Isa. 56:7), and in which the early Christians found the best of all Old Testament insights into what Jesus himself had taught and done (Isa., ch. 53). Let us look now a little more closely at the second section, chs. 40 to 55.

Perhaps a good way into it is through one of the memorable passages of the Nobel Prize-winning author John Steinbeck:

> I believe there is one story in the world, and only one. . . . Humans are caught—in their lives, in their thoughts, in their hungers and ambitions, in their avarice and cruelty, and in their kindness and generosity, too—in a net of good and evil. . . . We have only one story. All novels, all poetry, are built on this never-ending contest in ourselves of good and evil.[25]

The only problem in the world is the question of good and evil and our place in it. This is a particular problem for Christians and Jews. For we claim to believe that there is a God of goodness and justice in charge of it all. Why, then, is there so much heartache, disappointment, suffering? An Englishman wrote sometime ago: "I don't know what I believe, but I don't believe all this 'God is love' stuff. I've been in two world wars, been unemployed eighteen months on end, seen the missus die of cancer, and now I'm waiting for the atom bombs to fall." Why do some saints lie on beds of pain for years, while plenty of sinners enjoy the best of health? Why isn't the economic victory always to the honest, and the competitive race always to the righteous?

About five hundred and forty years before Christ, the Jewish people were asking questions like that. They thought chiefly in terms of themselves as a nation: Why had their nation been conquered and many of its people exiled to a strange land? What had happened to their God? They could believe for a while that he was punishing them for their sins, but when they saw that their conquerors were no better than they were, that answer couldn't permanently satisfy. In fact, imperfect as they were, morally and spiritually they were at least as good as their enemies! Yet they had been utterly crushed.

God's answer to their problem was given through an anonymous poet-prophet who is referred to as the "Second Isaiah." "His spiritual epic not only inflamed the faith of Israel, but surpassed all other writings of the Old Testament . . . in its influence on mankind." [26] It was given him to see that God was interested not only in the people of Israel but in all people. "No one contributed more . . . to the transformation of the national religion of Israel into a religion for all men." [27] The three universal religions in the world today—Judaism, Mohammedanism, and Christianity—are indebted to

his genius. Some of the most famous and familiar words
of Scripture were first penned by him:

Comfort, comfort my people, says your god. (Isa.
40:1.)

All flesh is grass, / and all its beauty is like the
flower of the field. The grass withers, the flower
fades, / . . . but the word of our God will stand
forever. (Isa. 40:6–8.)

He will feed his flock like a shepherd . . . and
gently lead those that are with young. (Isa. 40:11.)

They who wait for the Lord shall renew their
strength, / they shall mount up with wings like
eagles, / they shall run and not be weary, / they
shall walk and not faint. (Isa. 40:31.)

When you pass through the waters I will be with
you. (Isa. 43:2.)

How beautiful upon the mountains / are the feet of
him who brings good tidings, / who publishes
peace. (Isa. 52:7.)

For my thoughts are not your thoughts, / neither
are your ways my ways, says the Lord. (Isa. 55:8.)

The crown of his work, it seems to me, is the fifty-
third chapter. In it, in the hope that his people will become the ideal servant of the Lord, he phrases the deep-
est answer man has ever found to the problem of evil.
As we turn to it, let us remember that it is a poem. We
cannot pick it to pieces and expect to find its meaning.
If we try too hard to find its meaning, we will possibly
miss it altogether. A poem speaks more to our moods
than to our minds, more to our intuition than to our
logic.

Like all great minds, he began with something very simple and commonplace. He said, in effect, to his dis-spirited countrymen: *when trouble comes you can grimly "take it" or you can accept it.* Evil can be met either voluntarily or involuntarily. Sooner or later every one of us encounters sickness, or injustice, or tragedy. Homes are smashed by divorce; death takes loved ones before their time; friends let us down; we seek work and find none. Troubles come to us not only as individuals but as a nation. They may be the vicissitudes of defeat in war, or they may be the problems of the victors, which are hardly any less! Or they may be internal graft and corruption and treachery. Sooner or later we all have trouble, there's no getting around that. We can't always foresee it; but when it comes, we can take it in a bitter and rebellious way, or we can accept it with a will to try to make the best of a bad situation. That is where the prophet begins with his people in exile. He knows their sorrow and their grief. He knows that they need comfort and assurance. And he says that these things will come if the nation will fully *accept* the role forced upon it. He wants his people to serve the Lord not in spite of their condition but through their condition.

One of the books that was high on the best seller lists for months when it was published was *Karen,* the story of a girl born with the crippling malady cerebral palsy. "Doctor after doctor told her parents that she should be put in an institution and forgotten—that she was mentally backward, and would certainly never walk or talk." But Karen and her family did not spend their time bewailing the injustice of her plight. By a faith like that not found in Israel and unbelievable persistence they helped her to learn to walk, talk, read, and write. And they won more than a personal victory, for their efforts became the nerve center of a movement that is helping other similarly handicapped children. If you think this is just idle talk about the difference the attitude you take makes, I invite you to read that book.

When troubles come, accept them! So our prophet echoes the word of Jeremiah, who a few years before had advised the Jews exiled in Babylon: "Build houses and live in them; plant gardens and eat their produce. Take wives and have sons and daughters. . . . Seek the welfare of the city where I have sent you into exile, . . . for in its welfare you will find your welfare" (Jer. 29:5–7).

Another thing the prophet said to his people about the omnipresent problem of evil is a step higher: *when you accept evil you absorb it, and by absorbing evil you get rid of it.* Let me use a rather homely illustration. The mother of a certain small girl spent the best part of a day once in making a Halloween costume for the girl. Toward evening some incident upset the youngster and she was quite certain that she was being treated unfairly. The more she thought about it, the more it angered her and the more rebellious she became. When she went to bed her parting shot before the lights were turned out was, "I won't wear that dumb costume you made for me tomorrow." Anyone acquainted with a six-year-old's vocabulary will recognize that it was a remark fully calculated to cut to the quick. We are not far wrong—are we?—in saying that the youngster's attitude was an evidence of evil in the world. Her remark revealed her own bitterness and her intention to make someone else unhappy.

How can this evil be gotten rid of? To turn the light back on and give her a good spanking would most likely drive the rebellion deeper and perhaps make it more permanent. It might even produce problems, seemingly unrelated, for years to come. Or the mother might save the incident in her own mind with a resolve to get back at the child at the next opportunity. That would be bad for the parent, of course, and would also make the child unhappy, which in turn would lead to more remarks and perhaps overt actions of an even worse nature. Is it not clear that the way to get rid of that little bit of evil and to keep it from spreading or growing into something worse is for the mother simply to absorb it? She hears the remark but never says or does anything about it. She goes on as though nothing had happened. She does not let it poison her love for the youngster. She doesn't throw it in the child's face the next time something unpleasant happens. She absorbs it and it is ended then and there. So, says the prophet, does God deal with his children, and so also does he want his children to deal with one another.

Lift the principle up to a higher realm now. During World War II a Philippine woman and her husband were imprisoned by the invaders. Because they were in high political circles they were frequently questioned and then tortured when they refused to divulge information. She vividly remembers the night when they took her husband away for the last time. She found out later that they had beheaded him. After the war, there was an International Health Organization meeting in Manila. It was her duty to greet many of the visitors, among whom were three Japanese doctors. Graciously shaking their hands, she said later, was the hardest thing she ever did. "But," she added, "I know we must not hate and that there is no future in revenge." There you have it— God's way, the only way; to get rid of evil and prevent its growing is to absorb it completely.

Anyone can see where this leads, but no one more

clearly than the prophet. The next thing to note about his message to his people is that *it means suffering.* The people of the Lord, he said, would have to be a suffering people, "despised and rejected by men." If you try to absorb the evil of your children's cruelty, it will cause you inward anguish. If someone insults you and you do nothing about it, not only your pride will suffer but also your reputation in the sight of others. A nation that refuses to retaliate against its enemies, however great the provocation, will certainly suffer for it. Anyone who tries to absorb the evil of racial segregation will suffer for it. The husband or wife who tries to absorb the bitterness and recrimination and unfair accusations involved in a divorce will suffer for it.

This goes right against the grain. This is the reason we incline to say that religion is "too idealistic." We don't want to entertain the thought, even for a moment, that to do the right thing will mean that we will suffer. It is more than passing strange, however, that we should call the Second Isaiah "idealistic." Is he not most realistic? Has anyone ever said more plainly than he that the course he is advocating will mean sorrows and acquaintance with grief? It is we who are idealistic in thinking that life somehow was meant to cater to our comfort. Throw that theory against the clinical experience of humanity and see where it comes out! John Adams once read a line in a book by D'Alembert that went like this: "I am sometimes tempted to believe that God was at least as much in need of advice when he created the moral world as when he created the physical." To which the stern old Yankee statesman was moved to write in the margin, "Thou Louse, Flea, Tick, Ant, Wasp, or whatever Vermin thou art, was this Stupendous Universe made and adjusted to give you Money,

Sleep, or Digestion?" The idealists are the ones who think that life was designed for our convenience.

One of the moving scenes from the life of George Washington comes after the close of the actual fighting of the Revolution. There was a period of almost two years of terrible uncertainty about the future of the nation. As there was no peace treaty, the army had to be maintained in case of a resumption of hostilities. It is hard to keep morale in an inactive army, especially one that is underpaid when paid at all, poorly fed, and miserably supplied. A movement began snowballing for the army to take matters into its own hands and to redress its grievances by force. Even the officers were lending themselves to the idea. Washington called them together, not to rebuke or to chastise, much less to quell a righteous protest. But he had prepared a statement of the meaning of the war and the hopes for peace as they seemed to him which he wanted to read to them. "With no show of anger or offended dignity, but very gravely" he took the paper from his pocket. As he adjusted his spectacles he chanced to observe quite simply, "Gentlemen, you will permit me to put on my spectacles, for I have not only grown gray, but almost blind, in the service of my country." He need have said no more. They saw in him that the banishment of evil means suffering.

Isaiah's people could not believe what they heard from him (Isa. 53:1). They could not think that the arm of the Lord was openhanded in forgiveness rather than tightly closed in revengeful wrath. They never caught his vision; and neither have we. No nation—the Jews in antiquity nor America now—is willing to become the suffering servant of the Lord. Shall the vision go forever unrealized?

Ah, no. For if the prophet's people as a whole never

realized what he meant, there came One from them who did. There came One who turned his back on hatred and revenge, One who disappointed all fierce expectations, One who was "despised and rejected by men; a man of sorrows, and acquainted with grief." One who deserved more than any other to live, yet who accepted the injustice meted out to him, absorbing its evil, opening not his mouth. "He was wounded for our transgressions"—he suffered and died. But when we look at the history of humanity, "a single figure rises from the flood and straightway fills the whole horizon." There is the Savior, the Suffering Servant, and "the will of the Lord shall prosper in his hand; he shall yet see the fruit of the travail of his soul and be satisfied" (Isa. 53:10–11).

III

The third part of The Book of Isaiah may be from a disciple of the author of the second part. He too is a poet-prophet, but he is speaking to people in a little different condition than his mentor. It was given to him to see the promise of "new heavens and a new earth" (Isa. 65:17) which has helped both Jews and Christians to hold steady under persecution (cf. Rev. 21:1, 4) from the days of national degradation around 520 B.C. to the days of Antiochus Epiphanes (165 B.C.) and the Roman emperors down to Adolf Hilter and Mao Tse-tung.

The first thing we see in it is this: *all that God wants from us with respect to religious rites and ceremonies are those which contribute to righteousness*—kindness, social justice, ethical behavior. Fasting, for example, was highly regarded in the sixth century B.C. as a religious act; it was widely believed to be a very religious thing to do—just as, I suppose, it is widely believed in our

time that saying grace before meals is a religious thing
to do. The passage does not condemn fasting as a religious rite, just as I would not condemn the saying of
grace at the table. But it insists that fasting which does
not issue in ethical behavior is no good:

> Is not this the fast that I choose:
>   to loose the bonds of wickedness,
>   to undo the thongs of the yoke,
>   to let the oppressed go free,
>   and to break every yoke?
> Is it not to share your bread with the hungry,
>   and bring the homeless poor into your house;
>   when you see the naked [those who have no
>   clothing], to cover him,
>   and not to hide yourself from your own flesh?
> (Isa. 58:6–7.)

As with all the great prophets of the Old Testament,
this writer clearly sees that social justice is God's imperative—"the Lord saw it, and it displeased him that there
was no justice" (Isa. 59:15)—he says, while also realizing
that the fabric of ethical culture, righteous behavior,
social justice can seldom be maintained without religious rites, ceremonies, observances (cf. ch. 56:1–8). He
also clearly sees that not everything done in the name
of religious observance is worthy of the name because
it does not contribute to ethical conduct (cf. ch. 57:1–13).

That is worth remembering in our time. There is a lot
of pious singing these days about "standing on the
promises of God" by people who, as someone else has
put it, are really "just sitting on the premises." In God's
name what kind of abomination have we fallen into
when a man can't take a friend to church with him if

his friend happens to be a black? And, at the other extreme, as Sarah Patton Boyle (the Virginia-born author of *The Desegregated Heart*) found out, neither positive thinking nor any kind of humanitarian ethical culture society is going to be enough either! The only kind of religious rites that God is interested in—and which therefore will work over the long run—are those which issue in the fruits of the Spirit: love, justice, kindness, goodness, self-control!

Another thing that this passage says to us is that *there is no quick and easy way to arrive at the good community.* This part of the book comes from the time when the Jewish people had been allowed to return to their homeland after a couple of generations of exile in Babylonia. They came back with high hopes for restoring and rebuilding their national life. They soon ran into the dreary realities that always plague the execution of our visions, which always act as a drag on the accomplishment of our ideals.

Thanksgiving always reminds us of the high hopes and ideals that the Pilgrims, for example, had in coming to this new world. Yet, even before they landed, there was mutiny and dissension in the air and they had to draw up a compact—an agreement, a legal contract binding on all; the first child born in the Plymouth Colony was illegitimate, and before long they had a case of murder on their hands! There is a sort of tarnish that steals over our brightest resolutions! Some years ago one of the chaplains of World War II sent out Easter cards to his old outfit. On the front of the card was a German battlefield, labeled "Easter, 1945" and at the top was just one word, in large letters, "Remember?" Opening the card, you saw a family safe and happy at its fireside and a few more words: "Well! God did what you asked! He brought you safely home. Now, have you done what you promised?"

You don't need to have been in that outfit to know what he meant. On Easter, 1945, they had been in the thick of combat; more than one of them had vowed that if he ever got home alive, he would live a different kind of life; he'd straighten up, go to church, do the right thing, live a Christian life. And he meant it sincerely enough. But after the war was over, and he was back home, mustered out, the promise somehow lost its urgency and he either never started at all on the new life or he soon found it easier to slip back into the old.

That there is no quick and easy way to arrive at the good community, the society of civil rights for all, international cooperation, and the legitimate satisfaction of every other deep hunger of the human heart, is, of course, no excuse for not trying. It is no excuse for not using every means at our disposal to hasten the great day. On the contrary! That there is no easy way to it means that we must work all the more diligently to attain it, that we must expect to give ourselves to a long, drawn-out warfare of attrition rather than thinking in terms of lightning-like victories. As one wise woman put it a dozen years ago to another who had assured her that there were going to be changes soon in our terrible racial injustice: "Oh, no-o-o, not soon, not soon, honey chil'. There's sufferin' ahead." There is no quick and easy way to arrive at the good community; we are called to a long, arduous, discouraging kind of warfare.

A third thing we see when we look at this passage is *a vision of what God wants life on this earth to be.* One of its most striking sections—when one considers the grubby rubble in which Jerusalem lay at the time—says,

But be glad and rejoice for ever
 in that which I create;
for behold, I create Jerusalem a rejoicing,
 and her people a joy.
I will rejoice in Jerusalem,
 and be glad in my people;
no more shall be heard in it the sound of weeping
 and the cry of distress.
No more shall there be in it
 an infant that lives but a few days,
 or an old man who does not fill out his days. . . .
They shall build houses and inhabit them;
 they shall plant vineyards and eat their fruit.
They shall not build and another inhabit;
They shall not plant and another eat. . . .
They shall not labor in vain,
 or bear children for calamity. . . .
Before they call I will answer,
 while they are yet speaking I will hear.
The wolf and the lamb shall feed together,
 the lion shall eat straw like the ox;
 and dust shall be the serpent's food.
They shall not hurt or destroy
 in all my holy mountain,

Says the Lord.
(Isa. 65:18–25.)

A poetic way of saying that God's idea for life on this planet is that it should be without anguish or injury, that peaceful cooperation and harmony is the Creator's design for all his creation, the ideal toward which we should strive. The Christian way of putting it, of course, is to speak of the Kingdom of God. Both are ways of putting an idea that is in the minds of all good men:

they are religious terms for the world as it ought to be.

There is a type of person who thinks that religion should stay out of social relationships and political affairs. He usually talks about the main business of the church as being the saving of souls and repeats the cobwebbed fallacy that if we could just evangelize everyone individually, our social problems would be solved. But, as one of my teachers used to say, it is always possible to build a crooked wall out of straight bricks! This type, moreover, usually shows little interest in saving the social order or effecting those reforms in political and economic and racial affairs which "crib, cabin, and confine" —and sometimes damn—human souls. Such a person needs to read Isaiah! He needs to remember that the gospel says that God so loved the *world* that he sent Jesus that the *world* might be saved (John 3:16)! And he could profit from meditating on James 4:13 to 5:6, too!

Near the opening of this century an English preacher admitted that the leaders of the socializing labor movement in England were often crude, petulant, hard to deal with. But he said, "If I were in search of moral passion, I should know where to look." A *moral passion* for human welfare! Do you see that now in any of our political parties? Or in the National Association of Manufacturers or the Chamber of Commerce? Or the Medical or Bar Associations? Or the labor unions? I don't. Nor do I see it, I regret to say, in most of the churches. Most of the *moral passion* of our time has come from irregular sources, minorities, the youth, even the entertainers! It has come from the blacks, the Indians, the Chicanos, the Bob Dylans, Joan Baezes, Dick Gregorys, Ray Charleses! Whatever else you may say about Eldridge Cleaver or Malcolm X (and there are other things to say and to take into account), it must be admitted that they had *moral passion*. And that, gentle reader, threat that it may be to our domestic tranquillity, is closer to God's idea for human life than all the platitudes and caution and complacency we have baptized with the words "moderation" and "law and order" and "benign neglect" put together! It is to moral passion and ethical action that Isaiah, in all its parts, ever calls us.

Chapter 6

WHEN THE SAINTS
GO MARCHING IN

Moss Hart, the American playwright who died all too soon a few years ago, had a brother Bernard. They were not very much alike. Moss was elegantly handsome, famous, and wealthy. Bernie was an everyday sort of person, undistinguished in appearance and often only the stage manager for the shows his brother wrote or directed. Once they were working together on a new play; it opened in Washington to such resounding critical disdain and public aloofness that they closed it down after only a few performances. Then Moss went to work rewriting. The cast worked hard, hoping that his theatrical magic would come through. But the more he rewrote and the more they rehearsed the more despondent Moss got. One day, when he had reached the bottom, and Bernie knew it, Bernie said: "Don't worry, Moss. Please don't worry! We got out of Egypt. We'll get out of Washington."

Why do we mention this wry bit of Jewish humor? Because it casts a revealing light that helps us to understand the Bible better. We modern Americans are hard put even to begin to understand the strength that the

Jews have drawn from their own history when facing crises. If we did, we would understand The Book of Daniel better. Most of us remember at least some of the dramatic stories told there—Daniel in the lions' den, the fiery furnace, the handwriting on the wall, and so on. These stories are not history in the ordinary sense of the word. There is no reason to think that they ever actually happened, any more than there is any particular reason to think that the story of the good Samaritan actually occurred. That is a story with a moral, a meaning; and that is what these stories in Daniel are. But they are told against the backdrop of actual history, and they are told with the explicit purpose of strengthening the Jewish people to face a terrible period of history— persecution by the Greeks about one hundred and seventy years before Christ. The proof of their value is to be found in two facts: first, they survived; secondly, the Jews survived. There is something timeless and everlastingly relevant about them.

I

Like all good storytellers, the author worked up to a climax. The first story is, from our point of view, the least exciting. To some extent it is an introduction which sets the stage for them all. It tells about four young men who were carried away by the Babylonians when they sacked Jerusalem and took its leading citizens away to slavery and exile. They were young and healthy, so they were trained to be royal servants, and, naturally enough, they were given Babylonian names. We remember three of them by their Babylonian names: Shadrach, Meshach, and Abednego, but the fourth we remember by his Hebrew name, Daniel. Living in the palace, the boys were given "the king's rich food" and drink. And that is where the rub came in. They were Jews and knew that they ought not to eat anything that wasn't kosher. Kosher meat, for example, is slaughtered and handled in a special way in order to obey the Deutero-nomic injunctions about not allowing blood or milk to contaminate it. So the boys asked for a vegetable-and-water diet. But the official charged with their health, education, and welfare was afraid their health might suffer and then, of course, he would be held responsible. So they worked out a deal; he allowed them their special diet for ten days. At the end of the time they hadn't lost a pound; in fact, they were healthier than those who were eating the regular palace food. And when their training period was over, the king found they were smarter and more skillful than anyone else in the whole kingdom.

Well, the original purpose of the author was to show that faithful observance of the Jewish law pays. It was to encourage the faithful not to give up or surrender or compromise their religious ways. But what does it say to us?

One thing it says is that *human life needs structures of symbol and discipline.* We are not at our best or most effective when we are at loose ends. True freedom has a certain tension, a tautness about it; whatever it is, at its best we know it is not something slack or sloppy or vague.

No one has put this any better than Herman Wouk. He is an Orthodox Jew, every bit as orthodox as the author of Daniel could desire. And he tells of a letter from a long-time agnostic friend:

What is the *core* of being a Jew: to be different in living habits, or to practice a moral way of life

based on behavior toward other people? To imply
that in some significant measure the terrible problems of social existence on a crowded planet are
solved by refusing to eat lobsters seems irretrievably
petty to me.[28]

Who can dispute that kind of logic? And yet, Wouk
goes on with an analogy from his experience in the
Navy in World War II. He had been a midshipman for
a couple of weeks when he was slapped with a demerit
by an ensign for using the wrong words. As the officer
walked off, Wouk muttered to his buddy, "How will it
help beat the Japanese if I call a staircase a ladder?" He
learned to do so, however. One might debate whether
his learning had advanced the day of the surrender ceremonies any, yet it cannot be denied that the contribution he made to winning the war was in usefulness as a
naval officer, and that in part depended on his knowing
the lingo and belonging to the tradition—of working
from within a structure of symbol and discipline.

I read once of a member of the British Foreign Service
in the heyday of the Empire. He was assigned to duty
in a remote outpost on the very edge of the primeval
jungle. For months at a time he and his family would
see no other Englishman, no one but near-savages; the
amenities of civilization were few and far between. How
easy it is in that kind of situation to become a barbarian
oneself! The hand has a tendency to become the color
of the dye in which it works. What did they do? They
decided that every evening they would dress for dinner.
That, I submit, was not just an effete mannerism; it was
a little structure of symbol and discipline which helped
hold the jungle at bay.

So, at first glance, we may smile at a few Jewish boys
far from home refusing to eat food that wasn't kosher.

We may be a little disdainful of our Puritan forefathers with their grim Sabbaths and the Victorians with their frigid codes. But the question I put to you is this: What structures of symbol and discipline do we have? How do we maintain our identity as Christians in the midst of a non-Christian world? If we do not read the Bible every day, what do we do? If we do not have family prayers, what do we do? If we do not tithe our incomes, what do we do? Human life needs structures of symbol and discipline! If our society is sick, as many people are saying that it is, my guess is that nothing is more to blame than our failure to erect and heed some symbols of structure and discipline.

Then again, this old story says to us that *the men of the most usefulness to God are those of absolute devotion.*

When you run your mind over the gallery of great Christians, you cannot but be impressed that one of the few common denominators, perhaps the only thing they all had in common, is their absolute devotion. They were not quislings, compromisers, halfhearted men. They went all out. Do you remember that dramatic scene in Francis of Assisi's life where he strips off all his clothing so as to return to his earthly father absolutely everything that is his, so that he can render an absolute devotion to God? Do you remember how William Booth, as a teen-age boy, resolved to "go in for God" with everything he had? In later years someone asked Booth what the secret of his success was. The old general thought a moment, then said: "I will tell you. God has had all there was of me. There have been men with greater brains than I, men with greater opportunities; but from the day I got the poor of London on my heart, and a vision of what Jesus Christ could do with the poor of London, I made up my mind that God would have all of William Booth there was. And if there's anything of power in the Salvation Army . . . it is because God has had all the adoration of my heart, all the power of my will, and all the influence of my life."

Some years ago a minister was scheduled to be the speaker for the Religious Emphasis Week at the University of Mississippi. Then it was discovered that he was a contributor to the NAACP and his invitation was withdrawn. Whereupon some of the faculty became very restless, and at least one resigned. But most were placated by the chancellor's plea that this was not "the ditch to die in." And soon everything settled back to normal. Ah! "A ditch to die in." It is doubtless wise to choose one's battles carefully. When you are hunting, it is foolish to waste your ammunition on the squirrels. But the men who have been the most useful to God seem not to have been particularly careful about the ditches they died in. They seem intuitively to have recognized that for most of us choosing the proper ditch to die in is more of a rationalization, more of a succumbing to temptation, than anything else. Maybe if a few faculty members at Ole Miss had been willing to die metaphorically or professionally in that ditch in 1955, there would not have been forty-two civil rights murders in Mississippi in the next ten years! Maybe if Christians hadn't been choosing their ditches to die in so selectively for the last thirty years, a Black Power crisis might not be on our hands. Maybe if we had spoken out against and rooted out our American superiority toward Orientals, Red China might not now have the bomb (for some of their top experts were humiliated as students and even as professors in this country).

I am fully aware of the dangers of fanaticism and of

the atrocities that have been committed in the name of conscience. But few persons reading this book are in danger of becoming religious fanatics; no one of us is likely to follow his conscience too rigidly! Our danger, like that facing the Jewish people when Daniel was written, is that we will accommodate ourselves too readily to our culture. And the people who have been the most useful to God have never done that. They have stood out, rather, with a personal integrity born of an absolute devotion.

A wise housekeeper once pointed out one of the more discouraging aspects of that noble profession to a young bride. "Honey," she said, "housework's one thing there's no catchin' up with. You go to bed at night, everything's done, but while you're sleepin' sheets are wrinklin', dust is settlin', and stomachs are gettin' empty!" Just so. And in those other houses we live in, called character, the same thing is happening. Ideals are always getting wrinkled, the dust of the world is settling on our impulses to justice, our supply of decency and fairness is dropping. If we just let ourselves go, if we follow the path of least resistance, we lose something precious. No man ever was a Christian for very long without working at it! May God give us grace to use such structures of symbol and discipline as will build us up in the Christian life, and the devotion to his purposes which will make us useful to him!

II

Is there anyone who has not wondered what a dream may mean? Some dreams, to be sure, are clearly related to recent experiences, and we dismiss them without much further thought. But some dreams are mystifying, we do not understand them, try as we will to sort out their psychedelic impressions.

So it is not surprising that there have been a lot of theories about dreams. Scrooge, you may remember, thought that his dream about his dead partner Marley might be caused by indigestion. Some have thought that dreaming was a sort of defense mechanism to keep unpleasant thoughts from waking us up; recent researchers have discovered that almost everyone dreams all the time and that if we are not allowed to dream we cannot sleep. Freudian psychiatry holds that dreams are "the royal road to the unconscious reaches of the mind," and others have suggested that dreams may be a way of erasing unneeded information.

The ancients had their theories about dreams, too. Like modern researchers, they believed that important matters were revealed in dreams. For them, however, they were not the royal road to the human unconscious but the inside track to the divine consciousness; they were conceived as the vehicle by which the gods made known their intentions, and thus the shape of things to come. And of such is the story in the second chapter of Daniel.

Nebuchadnezzar had had a bad night; "his spirit was troubled, and his sleep left him." So he called in his advisers—wise men, astrologers, soothsayers, magicians—and asked their help. He may have forgotten, on awaking, the dream that troubled him so, because he asked them not simply to tell him what the dream meant, but what the dream itself was! That was a tough assignment; they had plenty of books to consult as to the symbolic meanings of various elements in dreams (copies of which archaeologists have dug up), but nobody had ever asked them before to read his mind and tell him what he had dreamed, and then its meaning! So, naturally, they stalled a little and tried to beg off. But the king was in a bad mood, accused them of conniving and corruption, and threatened to have them torn limb from limb. Still no one could show him his dream, and in a rage he "commanded that all the wise men of Babylon be destroyed."

Enter our hero Daniel. He and his friends were in the wise-man profession. Why they hadn't heard of the king's problem earlier the storyteller doesn't say, but it clearly accents the melodrama. They obtained a brief reprieve, just long enough for Daniel to have a dream of his own which revealed to him what the king's had been. So he went before the king to attempt the task that none other could do.

The king had dreamed, he said, of a great statue whose head was of gold, its chest and arms of silver, its midsection of bronze, its legs of iron, and its feet of clay. And as he watched, a huge boulder had fallen on the statue and smashed it to smithereens. Then the boulder itself got larger and larger, until it was a mountain that filled the whole earth.

So much for the dream. What it meant, he said, was this: King Nebuchadnezzar was the golden head; after him there would be other kings, each inferior to the preceding as silver is to gold, and bronze to silver, iron to bronze, and clay to iron. But finally the God of heaven would break them all to bits and establish his own kingdom. "The dream is certain, and its interpretation sure." It made sense to the king, so he "gave Daniel high honors and many great gifts, and made him ruler over the whole province of Babylon, and chief prefect over all the wise men of Babylon."

Why was the story told? It was told to demonstrate the

superiority of Jewish wisdom to heathen wisdom, and to show that God was about to smash the heathen empires. The author is talking about the rise and fall of the Babylonian, Median, Persian, and Greek empires. Since he and his readers were living under the Greeks, it was clear to them that he was saying that the Greek oppression was soon to end by divine intervention. But what is the significance of the story for us?

First of all, *this story holds a key to understanding Daniel aright*. Daniel has for a long time been a happy hunting ground for religious kooks and oddballs. It has fueled a lot of zany rockets, most of which, fortunately, have come down almost as fast as they went up. It has encouraged a lot of fortune-telling by Christians which has turned out to be as bad as that of the Babylonians.

The phrase that is the tip-off is this: "what will be in the latter days" (Dan. 2:28), and it indelibly marks Daniel as a piece of apocalyptic literature. Daniel is, in fact, the first great apocalyptic book; there are plenty of other examples of the same kind of literature in the four centuries bracketing the life of Jesus, but the only greater one, if indeed it is greater, is the book of Revelation in the New Testament.

Apocalyptic literature has characteristics as typical of it as poetry does, or as novels do. It always deals with the *eschaton*, the latter days, the end of the age of evil and corruption and the establishment of the day of justice and righteousness. It deals with the great Day when the saints will go marching in to their proper reward. It is the religious version of the statesman's Utopia, the theological equivalent of the philosopher's vision of a time of truth and harmony.

Another of the typical characteristics of apocalyptic literature is its use of deceptive meanings. It seldom

means what it at first seems to mean. A modern example
of the same sort of thing, involving The Book of Daniel
itself, appeared in Italy little more than a century ago.
Italy was in a revolutionary struggle to free itself from
the domination of Austria, and two words began to appear on walls and public buildings: *Viva Verdi,* "long
live Verdi." To the police of the Austrian imperial
power they seemed nothing more than the sign of public
enthusiasm for a young composer who had caught the
public fancy with an opera about Nebuchadnezzar the
king of Babylon. To loyal Italian patriots, however, the
words meant something far more stirring than that.
They saw in the opera itself a disguised version of Italy's
own troubles; and when the prophet sang, "Death to
the foreign tyrants!" every son of Italy was thinking
about the Austrians and not about the Babylonians. And
when they chalked VERDI on the walls the initiated
knew full well that the letters stood for the words *V*it-
torio *E*manuele, *R*e *D'I*talia—Victor Emanuel, King of
Italy.

Still another typical characteristic of apocalyptic literature is its use of what might be called "cartoon" language. Like a modern political cartoon on the editorial
page, it often distorts common objects in order to convey
symbolic meaning—a statue with a head of gold and feet
of clay, for example. Well before the 1968 Presidential
nominating conventions, you may remember, one of our
popular news magazines had a cover that showed some
jockeys lined up for their weighing-in before a horse
race. The jockey on the scale was clad in royal color—
purple; his face was caricatured but familiar—LBJ; and
his saddle had its handicap weights plainly labeled—
"war," "peace." Then there was a little jockey, almost
hidden, but in Irish green and with a Bobby Kennedy

nose and haircut. Romney was there, in "true blue," and Nixon in a checkered shirt recalling his famous dog. And so on. The title was, "Weighing in for '68," and the story, of course, was about the Presidential sweepstakes.

Knowing that Daniel is an apocalyptic book with caricatures like that saves one from a great deal of bad Biblical interpretation.

The story itself has at least one important truth for us: *it highlights the importance of seeing history steadily and seeing it whole.* This author had a remarkably comprehensive philosophy of history for his time; it did not include simply Israel (as the book of Deuteronomy, for example, does) but embraced all mankind. He puts history, to be sure, into what even then were conventional categories: a golden age, a silver age, a bronze age, an iron age, and lists them pessimistically in a descending or deteriorating order. But he introduces also the optimistic, hopeful note of a divine age, a "mountain filling the earth," what the New Testament calls the Kingdom of God, a conception that Christians have adopted but Jews have not; a conception that marks one of the basic differences between Christianity and Judaism.

This writer sees the coming of the Day of justice, peace, truth, righteousness, brotherhood, the day for which every good man hopes, the day without which there is little point to being a good man, after a long historical process, as the culmination of a succession of worldly empires. The history of any given people, the Jews, the Babylonians, the Greeks, the Americans, has its full significance, not in itself alone, but only in connection with those who have preceded and those who will come after them.

That ought to be a sobering and helpful thought for

us. Most of us see world history too much through the
lens of our own tradition. One year Jaroslav Pelikan, of
Yale University, was an ecumenical lecturer in my town.
He is one of Christendom's top authorities on the
Lutheran Reformation. He made a passing remark to
the effect that it was surprising how much light some
non-Christian, dogmatically secular Marxist historians
have been able to throw on the Reformation by sticking
strictly to economic and social factors! Granted, their
world view is a restricted one; so, he was saying, is our
own. They have something to say to our best scholarship,
even as ours has something to say to theirs.

The comprehensive view, moreover, saves us not only
from parochialism but also from discouragement. At any
given point in history the outlook is pretty bleak for
good men; it was that way for the Jews when Daniel was
written; it is that way now. And the temptation is to
give up your ideals and make any expedient compromise, on the one hand, or to swallow the half-truths of
the reactionary right on the other. To do either is to
give up the "good fight."

If one simply went by what one had seen in the paper
and on TV from Berkeley and other campuses in the
sixties, one might well be discouraged and alarmed.
Hundreds of students and nonstudents clearly were en-
gaged in activities that hardly seem calculated to im-
prove social health. But to see only that is to see things
through the zoom lens of a TV camera: one gets a very
high magnification of a very small part of the field of
action. At the same time that a few hundred protesters
were in the news, more than eight thousand U.C. students
were spending afternoons and weekends and vacations
working in disadvantaged areas—helping in schools,
neighborhood recreation, giving English lessons to Span-

ish-speaking people, building clinics. Before writing Berkeley off as a total loss, we ought to remember that it has sent almost twice as many volunteers into the Peace Corps as any other university! This story in Daniel is an attempt to see history as a whole, and that is always the path of wisdom.

III

According to the story in the third chapter, King Nebuchadnezzar had made a huge golden statue and set it up as an official object of worship. But Shadrach, Meshach, and Abednego, being devout Jews, did not bow down to it, and the news got back to the king. He hailed them into court, and threatened to burn them alive if they didn't obey. They stubbornly refused to do so, so he had them thrown alive into an overheated kiln of some sort, "a burning fiery furnace." The story says that it was so overheated that the soldiers who threw them in were burned to death just pushing the victims in! But then an amazing thing happened. The king could look in at the bottom and see that Shadrach, Meshach, and Abednego were not being burned. And there was a fourth Person with them, whose appearance was "like a son of the gods."

So the king called to them, and Shadrach, Meshach, and Abednego came out. They were examined and debriefed by the top scientists of the land and found to be unharmed in any way. They didn't even smell of smoke, so the king granted them minority rights, forbade anyone even to speak against their God, and promoted them in the civil service.

The chief purpose of the story was to show that *martyrdom is preferable to apostasy*. The Jews were quite literally being ordered to worship Greek idols, and the author was encouraging them to refuse even though they died for it. "Better dead than Greek!" was his motto.

The story also says that *God does not believe in anti-Semitism.* "At that time," we read, "certain Chaldeans came forward and maliciously accused the Jews" (Dan. 3:8). At one time or another that has been the story of the Jews not only in Babylonia, or under the Greeks, or in medieval Europe, or Hitler's Germany and Stalin's Russia, but also in the U.S.A. and your town.

Anti-Semitism seems to break out cyclically, as though it were caused by a virus which lies dormant for a while but which becomes more virulent with each epidemic. There is a lot of covert or latent anti-Semitism in American political life, as witness the popularity of the Know-Nothing Party a hundred years ago, the Ku Klux Klan, Father Coughlin, Gerald L. K. Smith, and the radical right today. There is a lot of covert or latent anti-Semitism in the social world of fraternities, lodges, and clubs, as witness their membership practices. There is a lot of covert or latent anti-Semitism in our vocabulary and our jokes. And there is a lot of covert or latent or blatant anti-Semitism in a great deal of what passes for Christianity, both Roman Catholic and Protestant.

But God does not believe in anti-Semitism. He believes that Jews are human beings, no better and no worse as a group than Babylonians, Greeks, Spaniards, Germans, Russians, or Americans. Although both Jews and Christians have tried to do it, he refuses to classify Christians as better than Jews, or vice versa. A few elections ago the news reporters tried to pin down General George C. Marshall as to his preference between Adlai Stevenson and General Eisenhower. Each had been his subordinate, and surely he had made a personal assessment of their relative merits. But all he would say was, "They are both my boys." So with God; we are all his "boys," and he doesn't believe in playing favorites. What he wants for each of us is a fair shake. And what he wants each of us to do is to give the other fellow a fair shake and never discriminate against him because of his ancestry, national origin, or religious convictions.

This old story says to us, furthermore, that *there ought to be some things* that a Christian will not do. These Jewish boys, far from home, are held up as heroes because for them there were some moral impossibilities.

What is there that you *would not do?* Every religious man has to make his own list. A lot of us have fudged a little here or there on a business deal. Would you own stock in or work for a firm that makes napalm if you knew for sure that napalm was being used against women and children? What is there that you *would not do?*

Life magazine once ran a notable editorial, well worth remembering now when so many people are disturbed about demonstrations. It was in its first issue after we bombed Hiroshima and it said:

> Our sole safeguard against the very real danger of reversion to barbarism is the kind of morality which compels the individual conscience, be the group right or wrong. The individual conscience against the atomic bomb? Yes. There is no other way.[29]

Every Christian ought to have his personal list of moral impossibilities. He ought to encourage others to have such lists, and he ought to respect their lists.

The story makes it clear that *faith is more than belief in spite of evidence; it is life in scorn of consequence.*

There have always been people who have tried to reduce religion to a belief in the unlikely. They sit along with Linus in the pumpkin patch year after year telling us that if only we'll believe sincerely enough, the Great Pumpkin will reward us. Whatever the evidence for evolution, they ignore it and equate religious faith with ignoring it. Whatever the evidence that the New Testament writers expected the bodily and visible return of Christ within the lifetime of men then living, they make the imminent "second coming of Christ" a fundamental article of faith. They equate faith largely with believing in spite of the evidence.

But real faith means living in scorn of consequence. There is a great line in this story where that comes out unforgettably. Shadrach, Meshach, and Abednego have heard the king's threat to burn them alive, but they courageously answer: "If it be so, our God whom we serve is able to deliver us from the burning fiery furnace; and he will deliver us out of your hand, O king. But if not, be it known to you, O king, that we will not serve your gods or worship the golden image" (Dan. 3:17–18). "Our God is able to save us"—that is really only a belief for which they could muster no conclusive evidence. But their faith goes farther than that: ". . . but if not"! That is real faith, a life of integrity and courage no matter what!

During the years when France was under the Nazi boot a man was marked for execution because he would not collaborate. Shortly before his execution he wrote these lines: "I should like my fellow countrymen to know that I am dying that France may live. I have made a last examination of my conscience and I am satisfied. If I had to begin over again, I would travel the same road. In a few moments I am going out to prepare for the tomorrows that sing." The tomorrows that sing! That is what this story is all about. And that is what Christianity is all about, too.

IV

At a shipboard governors' conference a communication once went astray. According to the reports the President had sent some instructions to one of the governors, but by some mistake the telegram was delivered to one of the opposite party who immediately made the astute political move of leaking the whole thing to the press.

The story in the fourth chapter of Daniel is cast in the form of a letter that would have had to go astray also. It is told as though it were a letter from King Nebuchadnezzar, and since it does not project a wholly favorable image of him, he would never have published it himself; it would have had to pass through hostile hands.

It tells about another of his dreams, a dream about a great tree in the midst of the earth. (The earth was believed to be just what it looks like to the unreflective eye—a flat disk with a blue dome for a covering. So a tree in the center could grow until it touched the outer edges and upward until it touched the inside of the dome.) It was a good tree, "its leaves were fair and its fruit abundant, and in it was food for all. The beasts of the field found shade under it, and the birds of the air dwelt in its branches, and all flesh was fed from it" (Dan. 4:12). But as the king watched, in his dream, an angel came out of heaven and gave orders for the tree to be cut down. Then a strange metamorphosis takes place. The dream is no longer about a tree but about a person gone mad, a man suffering from "insania zoanthropia" or lycanthropy, a kind of insanity in which a human being believes himself to be an animal and acts accordingly.

Naturally enough, the king wanted to know what the odd dream meant; and when none of his wise men could tell him, he called in Daniel. The thought of it dismayed even him for a moment, and the king had to reassure him. So Daniel went ahead. The great tree, he said, was the king himself: "It is you, O king, who have grown and become strong. Your greatness has grown and reaches to heaven, and your dominion to the ends of the earth" (Dan. 4:22); the cutting down of the tree meant his own fall from sanity. And, the story goes on, about a year later the king went off his rocker and "he was driven from among men, and ate grass like an ox, and his body was wet with the dew of heaven till his hair grew as long" as a hippie's and his nails were like claws.

So far as the author is concerned, the story was told to show that even the greatest of earthly powers is helpless before the God of Israel. His purpose, of course, was to encourage the faithful to stand fast against the wicked Greeks, who were arrogantly spreading themselves and their culture "like a green bay tree" (Ps. 37:35, KJV). Before long, he is saying, they would be cut down to size. And, we may add, they were. It is a powerful old story with lessons for our time as well as theirs.

Here was a man who was proud and didn't know it. The tree filling the earth and reaching to heaven was a perfect symbol for him. Nebuchadnezzar was as proud as a peacock of his kingdom and his accomplishments, and he left inscriptions so that future generations would know what great buildings he had built. "Is this not great Babylon, which I have built by my mighty power as a royal residence and for the glory of my majesty?"

(Dan. 4:30.) In his own vain imagination he thought he ruled the whole world and that everyone depended upon his largesse. Yet, when he dreamed about a pretentious tree that was cut down to size he had to ask someone what it meant! He never saw the likeness between it and himself until Daniel pointed it out.

Jesus once told a story about two men who went up to the Temple to pray. One was a devout and patriotic man, the other a corrupt collaborator with a foreign oppressor.

> The Pharisee stood and prayed thus with himself, "God, I thank thee that I am not like other men, extortioners, unjust, adulterers, or even like this tax collector. I fast twice a week, I give tithes of all that I get." But the tax collector, standing far off, would not even lift up his eyes to heaven, but beat his breast, saying, "God be merciful to me a sinner!" (Luke 18:11–12.)

And Luke tells us that Jesus told this story to those "who trusted in themselves that they were righteous." It was told to the good, respectable, religious, people and he was saying that they were proud and didn't know it!

That can happen to a nation. It was easy for us to see that General de Gaulle was proud to the point of arrogance; it is hard for us to believe that most of the world thinks that of us! Not long ago I glimpsed part of a television interview with the then president of Lions International. He lived in Puerto Rico and spoke with a South American accent. He told the interviewer that Europeans and Asians, not realizing that Puerto Rico is under our jurisdiction, often tell him just what they think about Americans. And what they think is not flattering. They think that American tourists look down their noses at non-Americans, boast about how much better things are in this country, and make vulgar displays of too much money.

A United States senator has given some lectures in which he maintains that our foreign policy, particularly with respect to Vietnam, bespeaks an "arrogance of power." By that he meant that we seem determined to go our own way, whether or not any other major nation in the world agrees with either our analysis of the situation or our prescribed remedy. Naturally enough his idea was not very popular in the administration of the time; but it was not popular in the Congress nor among the citizenry, either. About the same time, the American Friends Service Committee, which has had a long and honorable record of responsible participation in international affairs, issued a report. One of the things it said was:

> America . . . must become aware of the subtle and dangerous assumption that the United States can determine the course of the whole world, either through military power or economic power. . . . The fallacy of the *Pax Americana* is . . . conditioning our thinking.[30]

About the same time a Pulitzer Prize-winning historian, who has himself been involved in the higher levels of the Federal Government, was writing that we had trapped ourselves in a difficult dilemma because "of old illusions—the illusion of American omnipotence and the illusion of American omniscience." All of which are enough to make one wonder, at the very least, whether we may not be, like Nebuchadnezzar of old, blind to our own pride.

This story also underlines the conviction that *power is always more vulnerable than it looks or thinks.* There was that great, strong, growing tree—reaching to heaven and anchored deeply in the earth. Yet in a fraction of the time it had taken it to grow, it was cut down. There was the king—one moment strutting on the roof of his palace, with an empire at his command, and in almost the next moment he has slipped a mental cog and is exiled from human society. Here, to the author, was the Seleucid part of Alexander's old empire, an empire in itself, and one determined to stamp out every vestige of Jewishness within its borders. Against it was arrayed a handful of guerrilla fighters following old Mattathias and his sons. People were wondering what chance those guerrillas had against a powerful empire and the author was telling them that the empire was more vulnerable than they thought. Power—political, economic, military —is always more vulnerable than it looks or thinks.

The reason for that, I suppose, is that all things mortal are subject to a law as inexorable as the law of gravity—the law of change. Nothing in this world stays the way it is very long. The scientists sometimes work with atomic particles whose lifetime is only a fraction of a second. A man may live for threescore years and ten, more or less, but at seventy he's not exactly as he was at fifty or at twenty! A nation or an empire may last a few hundred years, but not unless it is flexible enough to change. Just about a hundred years ago Otto von Bismarck declared that Germany's problems could be solved only by "blood and iron." In a generation the Iron Chancellor unified the German people and created an empire ruled by a Prussian military cast. The Reichstag supported him unanimously. In a famous speech in 1888 he explained that his increasing military budgets were the best guarantees of peace. "That sounds paradoxical," to quote him exactly, "but it is true. With the powerful machine which we are making of the German army no aggression will be attempted." Yet that power was more vulnerable than he knew; modern historians say that "there has rarely been a statesman whose work lasted as short a time as did Bismarck's," and the German people twice within half a century of his death saw their tree of destiny cut down.

Ah, the vulnerability of power! The changeableness of all things mortal! One of the civil rights workers murdered in Alabama in recent years wrote a perceptive word shortly before his death.

> Reality is kaleidoscopic in the black belt. Now you see it and now you don't. The view is never the same. Climate is an affair of the soul as well as the body: today the sun sears the earth. Tomorrow, and yesterday, sullen rains chill bones and flood unpaved streets. . . . Light, dark, white, black, a way of life blurs, and the focus shifts.[31]

Reality is kaleidoscopic; nothing mortal is static, unchanging; so power is always more vulnerable than it looks or thinks. That is a word not only for Nebuchadnezzar, and not only to encourage the Jews; it is one for us to take to heart.

There was a novel a few years ago called *The Rabbi*. The hero falls in love with a Christian girl; he doesn't try to convert her, but she soon realizes that for them to marry would mean the end of his professional career. So, without telling him, she goes to another rabbi to seek instruction. He is not very sympathetic; he has seen other would-be converts. "What do you see among the Jews that makes you want to be one of us?" he asks coldly. "Don't you realize that Jews are persecuted . . . and despised . . . and cut asunder?" She turns to go. She admits that she doesn't think she could ever feel like a Jew and is unworthy to join a people who have suffered so much. "You feel *unworthy?*" he asks; and then, suspiciously, "Who told you to say that?" No one had told her to say that; she said it because she felt it. So the old rabbi has to grant her request, because there is an old tradition that if anyone has been told what it means and says "I feel unworthy to be a Jew," he must be accepted immediately for conversion. Well, that is more than a secret password, so to speak, to an ancient faith. The attitude behind those words is poles apart from the attitude of Nebuchadnezzar and all other proud manipulators of power. "I am unworthy. . . ." That is the only password to a better life and a better world for us all.

Chapter 7

FROM ETERNITY
TO HERE

IN MANY WAYS The Gospel According to John is the most distinctive of the Gospels. The other three show clear traces of interdependence, but this one stands alone. John seems the product of a different time and addressed to different people. In no place is the contrast greater between John and the other Gospels than in the opening passage. Although the other Gospels move in the direction suggested by the once-popular book and movie *From Here to Eternity,* beginning with the earthly facts of Jesus' life and work and moving to a climax in his resurrection, John moves "from eternity to here." It begins not with the here and now of human history but with the far-off eternities of divine purpose: "In the beginning . . . " (John 1:1). And its chief purpose is to show how the eternal divine purpose has been made plain in the here and now of mortal existence.

Let us begin our examination with the famous "prologue," the first eighteen verses which serve the same function in this Gospel as the birth stories do in Matthew and Luke. That is, they tell us that Jesus is the incarnation of love, the projection of the divine personality who is love, God's "yes" to human existence.

I

The first thing to note is that *Christianity is intellectually respectable;* it is philosophically defensible. This passage is replete with and addressed to Greek philosophical ideas; the "word" was a favorite concept for relating Greek and Hebrew thought, the philosophical and the religious. Its use here is plainly an indication that this Gospel is one of the first "apologies" (intellectual defenses and justifications) of Christianity. The author is concerned with making Christianity acceptable to the most alert and informed minds of his time.

That seems to me to be worth noting, because most of us, I think, wish to be "intellectually respectable." We do not wish to be superstitious. We do not want a religion which, as Rufus Jones once put it, has no need for anything above the collar button! We see no particular virtue in being naïve or credulous. With John Wesley we say that "it is a fundamental principle with us that to renounce reason is to renounce religion, that religion and reason go hand in hand, and that all irrational religion is false religion." [32] We want a faith that can go into the philosophical arena with no holds barred and give a creditable account of itself. As Bishop Ensley once put it, "there are not a few able men and women who are out of the Church today, because in their youth they were indoctrinated with piffle, things that any intelligent mind would revolt against." [33]

When I say that our faith is intellectually defensible I mean that it makes sense. It may not be the only way to account for all observable phenomena, but it is a

self-consistent way of doing so. I read something by a
competent, if amateur, musician a while ago that went
like this:

> When you hear [the dominant seventh chord] you
> . . . know, even though you may not know any-
> thing about music, that it leads to something
> else and if someone doesn't play what it leads to,
> namely the tonic C major chord, you will go crazy,
> because the unresolved seventh chord leads into
> something else and it is not fulfilled until that
> great C major chord is sounded. You are kept in
> complete suspense until the chord is struck, and
> once it is, you are given the most perfect musical
> satisfaction.[34]

As far as I am concerned, Christianity does that for my
intellectual questions. There are enough uncertainties
and perplexities to drive a person crazy unless they can
be resolved in some great C major chord. And the being
and purposes of God as revealed in Jesus Christ our
Lord are such a chord for me; I find final intellectual
satisfaction in the concept of the Ultimate being personal, a Being to whom we can say as he taught us,
"Our Father."

This prologue to The Gospel According to John also
tells us that *Christianity is a materialistic religion.* I
imagine that sounds a little strange. Preachers are more
accustomed to exalt the spiritual and look down upon
"materialism." I am not, of course, using the word in
the low sense of meaning that material stuff is the all-in-
all of the universe. I am using it to mean that Christianity recognizes the reality and importance of the
worldly. Christianity is not some vague and nebulous
notion that the world as it appears to our senses is mere
"error of mortal mind." On the contrary! It asserts that

God sent his son to save *the world.* (John 3:16.) It appreciates and respects its reality to the utmost by asserting that the "Word became flesh and dwelt among us" —the Power and Purpose which holds the stars in their courses by invisible mathematical laws is not alien to the very visible and material flesh and blood of human life. As one of our journalists put it a while ago, there is a sign on earth's front porch which says, "God Almighty slept here."

A neurotic has been defined as a person who builds castles in the air; a psychotic is one who lives in them. And a psychoanalyst collects the rent! Christianity contends that our earthly home is not an air castle of imaginings or delusion. The rent we pay is for a real dwelling. As Archbishop Temple once put it:

> It may safely be said that one ground for the hope of Christianity that it may make good its claim to be the true faith lies in the fact that it is the most avowedly materialistic of all the great religions. It affords an expectation that it may be able to control the material, precisely because it does not ignore it or deny it, but roundly asserts alike the reality of matter and its subordination. . . . By the very nature of its central doctrine Christianity is committed to a belief in the ultimate significance of the historical process, and in the reality of matter and its place in the divine scheme.[35]

Nikos Kazantzakis, the author of historical novels such as *The Greek Passion* and *Freedom or Death,* was a child when the Turko-Cretan bloodbath of 1889 broke out in his native land. Every morning on his way to school he had to pass a tree where the Turks were wont to hang Cretan patriots. The first time he saw a dangling corpse, half stripped of clothing and with a greenish

tongue sticking out grotesquely, it made him almost
sick with fright. As he tried to hurry away, his father
took him by the hand and ordered him to approach the
corpse with his eyes open and touch its cold foot. Then
the older man said simply, "This man died for freedom."
I know that is not a very pleasant account; but it is no
more grimly realistic than the Gospels. If we didn't
read them with a saccharine glazing of "spirituality,"
we'd come a good deal nearer to understanding what
they are all about. And we'd understand what Black
Power and the poverty marches are all about. Christianity is a materialistic religion.

Furthermore, this prologue tells us that the purpose
of God, as seen in Jesus Christ, is the same as his purpose in Creation: *to give life.* "In him was life, and the
life was the light of men." If there is one word that is
the theme of The Gospel According to John, that word
is life, life "abundant," life "eternal," life "everlasting,"
—rich, free, full, complete. The word "life" occurs more
times in this one Gospel than in the other three put
together.

Broadly speaking, two ideas prevailed among the Jews
with respect to life. On the one hand, there were the
Pharisees, who thought that the real life was all in the
future, following the resurrection. And, on the other
hand, there were the Sadducees, who thought that the
present mortal life was the only one there was; life, for
them, was all in the present. These two ideas are still
widely held. There are persons—even in the name of
Christianity—who think that the only life worth talking
about is the one in some future heaven. And there are
those who think that the only life is the one of sensuous
indulgence; "live it up a little," is their slogan. But
eternal life is something else again. It is "a present ex-

perience of fellowship with God" conditioned by ethical obedience to the law of love. The fixed, unchanging purpose of God is to give us eternal life now.

Now that is good news, because if there is anything we all want, it is life. We want physical life. We spend millions every year on hospitals, medicines, research, and doctors to prolong physical life. We rejoice that our life expectancy is so much more than it was a generation or two ago. In one community I knew a man who hired three nurses and a physician and built a home for them near his own so that he could have constant care. He wanted physical life as long as possible! We want emotional life. When our emotions are battered and storm-tossed we are abnormal and depressed. We want mental life, and we build schools and universities as the guarantors that we shall have it. We all want life. In a modern novel a child asks an aged grandfather how life has seemed to him. "Like a glass of cool water, my child," replies the old man. "And are you still thirsty, Grandfather?" "Woe to him," cries the gray-bearded patriarch, as though he were pronouncing a curse, "woe to him who has slaked his thirst."

In our passion for life, however, we often overlook its basic condition. Life comes only from life; its maintenance is dependent upon a living relationship to its source. Flowers in a vase are beautiful, but they are no longer alive. They have been cut from the source that gave them life. The basic condition of life is a vital relationship to its source. So the basic condition of eternal life is a vital relationship to its Giver. Cut yourself off from him, and your life is really gone whether you know it or not.

The Bible is often its own best interpreter. Here, then, is a word not from The Gospel According to John but from Paul: "For it is the God who said, 'Let light shine out of darkness,' who has shone in our hearts to give the light of the knowledge of the glory of God in the face of Christ" (II Cor. 4:6). That is as good a summary of this passage as you will find! *Light*—the ideal of the Jew. *Knowledge*—the ideal of the Greek. *Glory*—the ideal of the Roman. All that the ancient world wanted and needed, all that the modern world needs, is to be found here: "the light of the knowledge of the glory of God in the face of Christ."

II

There is an old story about a man being initiated into a monastic religious order. He was taken directly to a cell furnished with only the simplest and barest of necessities. He was told that the first requirement for a man entering this order was seven years of meditation. Once a day someone would pass some warm milk in, but other than that he would have no interruptions. At the end of the seven years he was taken before his spiritual superiors for examination. "What," they wanted to know, "have you been meditating about?" The man could hardly talk, but with a finality born of long thought he managed to whisper, "I like *cold* milk."

That story appeals to us in part, at least, because it belittles an element of religion with which we have had little experience and which we habitually tend to minimize: mysticism. Western Europeans are not a very mystical people: even the Beatles could stand an Indian guru only for a little while! We Americans classify "mystical" as just about the opposite of "practical," and we pride ourselves on being, above all, a practical people. We are activists, and mysticism seems terribly passive.

There is a sense, however, in which I surmise that most of us have at least a touch of the mystical. While we may not go in for utter separation of religion from life, while we've never had any trances or visions, while we do not indulge in esoteric practices aimed at totally submerging ourselves in Deity, *we do have moments when we feel invigorated or transformed or uplifted religiously*. Sometime ago an eminently practical businessman paid a church about as fine a compliment as I can imagine. He said that he had been interested in hi-fi for years and has a set of components in his home in which he finds a great deal of pleasure. The ultimate test of high fidelity, he said, is whether or not it gives you a sense of presence—a feeling that the musicians are right there, that you have direct and immediate aural perception. Then he said: "That's what happens when I come here to church. I get a sense of Presence—the window, the choir, the sermon are just the equipment through which I sense God." If you are one who has ever had an experience anything like that, or who knows that such things do happen to some people, then the question as to whether or not the mystics are mistaken is not so quickly and easily answered.

In the last analysis, I suppose it depends upon what is meant by the word "mystic." If it means some devotee who "loses himself in the abyss of the Godhead as the drop of water is merged with the ocean," then I would say that mysticism is mistaken. If it means some sort of union with God by sacramental means by eating "the flesh of the Son of man" and drinking his "blood" in some formal rite such as Pope Paul has recently affirmed of the Roman Mass (with all its antecedents in animal sacrifice, sacred meals, and pagan mystery religions), then I would say that mysticism is mistaken. (Even Luther could not get beyond such a semimagical, superstitious view of the Communion service—he insisted that "this is my body" must be taken to mean that when the believer is receiving the bread and wine of Communion, God is present in some way which he is not at other times.) *But if "mystic" means a person whose sense of the presence of God is so acute, so real and immediate, that you can say that his life not only revolves around God but radiates godliness,* I would say that it is basic Christianity, for this is the mysticism of Jesus according to John's portrait—a person whose sense of the presence of God was so acute and immediate that his whole life revolved around, radiated from, and was the instrument of, God. "My teaching is not mine, but his who sent me." (John 7:16.) "The Father who dwells in me does his works." (Ch. 14:10.) "What I say, therefore, I say as the Father has bidden me." (Ch. 12:50.) "I proceeded and came forth from God; I came not of my own accord, but he sent me." (Ch. 8:42.)

This mystical union between Jesus and God often troubles and confuses readers of this Gospel because it causes the line between the human and the divine to become very faint indeed, with the result that it is easy to fall into the confusing mistake of identifying Jesus and God. It is therefore very important to note that classic, orthodox, Christianity has never said: "Jesus is God." It has said that Jesus is the *incarnation* of God; it has said that "God was *in* Christ"; it has said that in Jesus there was *manifested* the Second Person of the Trinity. It is important to note that neither in this nor in any of the other Gospels does Jesus speak of himself as God: he always subordinates his relationship. "Why do you call me good?" he asks in Mark. "No one is good

but God alone." (Mark 10:18.) "The Father," he says
here in John, "is greater than I." (John 14:28.)

This mystical union between Jesus and God does
mean, however, that *for all practical purposes Jesus has
for us the value of God.* For all practical purposes he
who has seen Jesus knows what God is like. A life with
a clear sense of the presence of Jesus, revolving around
him, radiating from him, will be morally and spiritually
like a life with a clear sense of revolving around, radiating from God. John calls us to exactly the same relationship with Jesus that Jesus enjoyed with God. "I am
in my Father, and you in me, and I in you." (John
14:20.) In one of his prayers in this Gospel Jesus says,
"I . . . pray . . . that they may all be one even as
thou, Father, art in me, and I in thee, that they also may
be in us." (John 17:20, 21.) Just as Jesus was sent, so
are we: "As the Father has sent me, even so send I you"
(John 20:21). *In John's thought, the mystical relationship of the believer to Jesus is described as precisely the
same as that of Jesus to God and is expected to produce
similar results.*

This is so practical a mysticism that it is very hard! It
is much easier to believe that Jesus is the Son of God
than for us to act like sons of God ourselves, walking as
he did with dignity and grace amid the confusion and
disappointments of life! It is easier to believe that Jesus
was a revelation of the divine love than to be so closely
attuned to him that we ourselves are persons through
whom that love shines! It is easier to believe that Jesus
raised Lazarus from the dead than to be so like him that
we give people new life! It is easier to talk about Jesus as
the Prince of Peace than it is to be a peacemaker at
home or in the family of nations! But this is the true

Christian mysticism: to be a person so attuned to Jesus that one's life revolves around and spontaneously radiates the will of God as his did.

There may well be a question in your mind: *Do we need Jesus as an intermediary?* If Jesus is not God, why don't we simply do as he did and attune ourselves directly to God? This is the serious question of both the Jew and the Unitarian. And I think (despite John 14:6) that theoretically we cannot argue with them; we cannot insist that the only possible mystical connection with God is through Jesus; we can believe that it is the best possible. The New Testament itself tells us that we can be as godly as Jesus himself. In him, it says, "the whole fulness of deity" dwelt bodily (Col. 2:9); but it also says that we too "may be filled with all the fulness of God" (Eph. 3:19). Theoretically we need no intermediary, we can make it on our own.

But, for practical purposes, *we do better under Jesus' inspiration and guidance.* That is what this author had discovered, and whoever discovered a true principle without pressing its application too far? That is why he traces our mystical relationship to God through Jesus rather than with absolute logical directness. One of my professors once used what I thought was a very illuminating analogy. He noted that when it comes to living a godly life there are always some failures, people who for one reason or another miss the meaning of it all and by any human evaluation, at least, would have to be flunked. Then there are a lot of people who don't do anything particularly wrong, but nothing particularly right either: they never rise to any particular achievement, they are content to muddle along and be as good as the next fellow. They are the class average and get about a C grade. But there are some who do better, try harder, accomplish more in the way of character—the B student—and at the very top are those who deserve an A.

One of our century's A students, one of the great and real mystics of the twentieth century, Albert Schweitzer, put it this way:

> He comes to us as One unknown, without a name, as of old, by the lake-side he came to those who knew him not. He speaks to us the same word: "Follow thou me!" and sets us to the tasks which he has to fulfill for our time. He commands. And to those who obey him, whether they be wise or simple, he will reveal himself in the toils, the conflicts, the sufferings which they shall pass through in his fellowship, and, as an ineffable mystery, they shall learn in their own experience who he is.[36]

In elevation, both of thought and of meaning, that is the true Christian mysticism!

III

A friend of mine was a guest on a cruise on Puget Sound, and as the last glow of the sunset was leaving Mt. Rainier and the darkness on the Sound was deepening, the skipper asked his guest if he would mind taking the wheel for a while. The skipper assured him that the craft was on course for Tacoma and that all he had to do was to pick out a light directly ahead and keep the bow of the vessel pointed toward it.

As far as the novice was concerned, all went well. But when the skipper came up from below he could see that the craft had changed direction and he wanted to know why. The innocent answer of the helmsman was that he was still heading for the same light he had been when he had taken over. "Man," sighed the skipper, almost in unbelief, "your light is a ferryboat and you have been following it across the Sound!"

Everyone needs a fixed point by which to steer, and every wise man tries to choose *truth* as his point of reference. But truth is seldom a simple or obvious thing. Many a man has followed a ferryboat, thinking it was a light on shore! One of the subtle temptations of life is to make decisions, assuming that they are oriented toward truth, without really going to the effort to be sure that they are.

For a long time truth has been expendable in matters of statecraft and diplomacy. When Jesus was standing before Pilate and told him that he had come "to bear witness to the truth" (John 18:37), that bureaucrat, with the might of the Roman legions at his right hand and the prestige of the Empire at his back, had a cynical rejoinder, "What is truth?" That seems to be the style, right through Machiavelli, Napoleon, Stalin, Hitler, Tojo, and the CIA. But it is worth noting that the truth Pilate scorned snuffed him out like a candle, while the centuries have given the man who stood for truth a name above every name.

This Gospel has an unusual interest in truth. It uses the word itself twenty-five times, whereas the other three Gospels use it only three times altogether! The Johannine literature taken as a whole uses the word about half the total number of times it is used in the New Testament. It is not afraid of truth; on the contrary, it is sure that the truth will make us free (John 8:32). Let us look now at some of the criteria for knowing the truth.

As a general rule we moderns apply two criteria in the search for truth. The first is *the scientific method:* Can it be tested and demonstrated to our senses in a controlled experiment? If so, it is true. So Einstein's theory of relativity was not really accepted until an eclipse, and now other natural phenomena, made it possible to test it that way. And his unified field theory, which he felt he had demonstrated mathematically, has not yet gained common currency because, as he sadly admitted before his death, he had not yet found "a practical way to confront the theory with experimental evidence."

Our other ordinary standard for determining truth is the test of *practical results*. Does it work? If so, "It's good enough for us." There is a scene in Mark Twain's *A Connecticut Yankee in King Arthur's Court* where the practical American sees a holy man swaying rhythmically in mystic devotion and finally figures out a way to hook up the power thus generated to a sewing machine! Unless something produces useful consequences, we have our doubts about it.

Now no one should minimize these avenues to truth. The scientific method has disclosed great stretches of reality to us. In my judgment scientists are God's servants, like Cyrus of old, whether they know it or not. Their truth is his truth. And the pragmatic test? Jesus himself told us that a tree is to be known by its fruits.

But I would urge upon you the necessity of additional standards. There are areas of life not covered by the scientific method nor accurately judged by mere practical results. Here, for example, is a line from Maurice Herzog, the leader of the expedition that conquered the previously unscaled Himalayan peak of Annapurna. The triumph had been won at the cost of great effort, tragedy, and exhaustion. And it cost him—through frostbite—all his toes and fingers. Recuperating in the

hospital, he wrote: "In my worst moments of anguish
. . . I saw that it was better to be true than to be
strong." How are you going to test a statement like that
scientifically? Or there is the idea that Jesus' mother
was carried up bodily into the skies. It "works" very
well for Pope Paul, but it doesn't work at all for me!
Testing hydrogen bombs in the South Pacific may have
been an excellent scientific experiment, but such a
program may not have worked at all in making friends
for us in Asia or in the rest of the world, or it may have
worked very well in the short run and yet may prove to
be a disaster in the long run.

What is truth? If we're to answer that, we need some
tests besides the scientific method and mere practical
results!

One additional way to identify truth is its *recognition
by sensitive minds*. "Every one who is of the truth
hears my voice" (John 18:37)—that is, he recognizes intuitively its authority. When a sensitive mind, either by
direct intuition or after a long period of disciplined
analysis or by both, is "satisfied," then its conclusion
has a claim to be respected as truth. Wallace Nutting,
the eminent authority on American colonial antiques
once put it this way: "The standard of beauty is the
recognition of it by the noblest minds." Why is the Taj
Mahal or the Parthenon or the *Mona Lisa* beautiful?
Because each has a proportion, a form, a texture, a color,
a combination of something-or-others that is readily
recognizable by minds sensitive to beauty! So with
truth. Great minds have an insight into reality that the
rest of us lack; and one of the ways for us to find truth
is to follow their lead.

We ought to follow the lead of the most sensitive
persons. Israel had her Moses and Isaiah. Greece had her

Plato and Aristotle. England had her Shakespeare and Milton; Germany, her Kant and Goethe; the United States, her Emerson and Lincoln. If Germany had listened to Immanuel Kant, with his dream of perpetual peace, instead of to Bismarck and Hitler, she would not twice in this century have become a no-man's-land. If Italy had listened to Dante instead of to Mussolini and if Japan had heard Kagawa instead of Tojo, neither would have felt the conqueror's boot. "If India had listened to Gandhi she would not be . . . divided. . . . If Russia had listened to Tolstoi instead of Lenin she would not be the menace to the world's peace she is today. . . . If America had listened to Lincoln she would not have bled herself almost white in a Civil War that still divides our country; if we had listened to Woodrow Wilson it might be there would have been no second World War" [37] or iron curtain or cold war or Vietnam. If we had listened to Roland Hayes or Countee Cullen forty years ago, or Martin Luther King ten years ago, our cities might not now be armed camps.

The intuition that we have been discussing lies at the basis of all knowledge. But it is not by itself an adequate criterion of truth. One must have a way of distinguishing genuine intuition (in oneself and in others) from a mere rationalization of personal desire. How was a German to know that Kant should be followed rather than Hitler? How could we have known that Wilson rather than Borah was right? So another test must also be applied, *the test of coherence*. That which is held to be true must fit in consistently with everything else recognized as true. Any given truth is necessarily positively related to all other truths.

Sir Percy Spender, onetime Australian ambassador to this country, once insisted that "peace depends . . .

upon understanding." No one will quarrel with the truth of that. He went on to tell what Australia was doing to provide a home for the homeless refugees of other lands. During the question period a black asked if Negroes, Orientals, or other non-Caucasians were being admitted to Australia. "No," said the diplomat, "we are trying to build a homogenous country." Well, you cannot hold to both points in the name of truth. If peace depends upon understanding, then it cannot be had by deliberately excluding some people from a nation on the grounds of racial ancestry. Understanding does not come that way! The policy is not true because it is not coherent with other accepted truths.

Truth coheres—it sticks together. How is a phony alibi story recognized by the police? By finding that it doesn't "hang together." How is religious belief to be tested for truth? By the way it hangs together with other truths. Eighty or more years ago, when many were alarmed by Darwin's ideas of evolution, Dr. James Woodrow, an uncle of Woodrow Wilson and a staunch Christian, was gladly accepting and teaching the new revelations in natural science. Was he afraid that it would destroy Biblical faith? No. "God's work and God's word," he said, "cannot contradict each other." When truths appear to be paradoxical it means that we have not pursued either or both far enough, that there is an undisclosed reality someplace farther on. Coherence is the test of truth.

Truth, moreover, as this Gospel rightly sees, *is a matter of being*. "I am the way, the truth, and the life." The true nature of anything is to be understood in terms of its highest being.

It is more important to *be* someone than to have something. It is more important to *be* someone than to know something. It is more important to *be* someone than to believe something. And it is more important to *become* someone than to be someone. Do you remember how Kipling's well-known poem "If" closes? After a noble enough catalog of life's hazards the supreme promise to him who overcomes is not in terms of getting but of being:

> Yours is the Earth and everything that's in it,
> And—which is more—you'll be a Man, my son![38]

So with the New Testament. It does not dwell much on man's present condition; it hurries over that to proclaim what we shall be. It does not continually harp on the condition of the old man; it urges us to put on the new man! It reveals the truth about human nature not in the likeness of a "fallen" Adam but in the likeness of a risen Christ!

The highest truth, in other words, is personal. "Grace and truth came through Jesus Christ." (John 1:17.) The best key to the universe is not an abstract mathematical principle, useful as that may be, nor a great impersonal nature, but a supreme person. When Paul was writing to his friend and protégé in the Christian gospel, Timothy, he was held in a cell in "death row" and knew that each day might be his last. What did the great apostle have to say about truth? He put it in terms of personal being, "I know *whom* I have believed" (II Tim. 1:12). He didn't know the truth about tomorrow any more than you or I. There were plenty of other things of which he was ignorant, even as we are and always will be. He didn't know *what* to believe about a lot of things, but he knew *whom* to believe.

There is a story about "the existential umpire." Three umpires were discussing their trade. One of them claimed that he called them as he "saw 'em," which surely is to be desired. The second, perhaps less modest, asserted, "I call 'em as they are." And that, surely, is a spirit worthy of emulation. But the third was the most realistic of them all, "They aren't anything," he said, "until I call 'em." Truth, even objective, factual truth, is really nothing but an abstraction until it is passed through the filter of human personality, and that is why this Gospel can claim that Jesus Christ is not only way and life but also truth.

IV

I want to deal now with a matter that relentlessly presses itself on the thoughtful reader of John's Gospel, a matter that I have touched on a time or two earlier but not in any conclusive way. It is a matter that has raised debate and controversy time and again in the church, a matter that every generation seems to need to put into a slightly different form, a matter that Jesus himself raised (in The Gospel According to Matthew): "Who do men say that I am?" (Matt. 16:15). Peter, born and raised a Jew, answered that he was the Messiah, an answer that spoke his language and met his need. But, before very long, there were those for whom the word "Messiah" had little, if any, meaning, and the word was translated for them into Greek: "Christ." Translation is always a tricky business at best and there is a sense in which one might almost say that the whole Gospel According to John is an attempt to fill that one word with content, to define it in a way both understandable and meaningful to a second generation of believers.

And, of course, the process has never stopped. "Who do men say that I am?" Peter answered, "Messiah"; John

answered, "Logos"; and every creed ever written has
given a new answer: "born of the Virgin Mary," "gift of
the Father's unfailing grace," "Light of Light," "Very
God of Very God," "one substance with the Father,"
"God manifest in the flesh."

Through the years, to be sure, the church has gradually realized that much of the verbiage boils down into
broad areas of agreement: generally speaking, all Christians believe in the incarnation (or, in more popular
language, in "the divinity of Christ") and all believe that
he is in some way the key to forgiveness, reconcilation,
atonement. But, if there are two main strands of theological thought among us, the one clustering around the
word "ecumenical" and the other clustering around the
word "evangelical," it must be said that genuine agreement beyond these broadest of outlines is probably
harder to find on this point than on any other. It is the
watershed in Christian thought.

Let me say, therefore, that I am not particularly interested in changing anyone's convictions in the matter.
I am interested in helping, rather, those who may feel
confused by the whole discussion, who could not answer
right now with any personal assurance the age-old question, "Who do you say that I am?"

Let us look at a familiar line from John: *"I and the
Father are one"* (John 10:30). You will see at once that
there is more than one possible meaning to that. It could
mean unity, oneness, in the sense of *absolute identity,*
"I" and "the Father" being two different names for the
same person, just as I might say to a stranger looking for
Raymond E. Balcomb, "I and he are one." Then again,
it could mean unity in the sense of *will, purpose, plan,*
just as an international negotiator might say, "The President and I are one," meaning: "If you talked to him

personally and directly, he would say the same thing I have said; his policy is mine; I am doing what he told me; he who has seen me has seen the President." Once more, it could mean unity in a third way similar to this second, yet deeper and more comprehensive—unity in the sense of the marriage bond when we say two persons have become one. That is, they are united in *the most intimate and meaningful and expressive and binding* ways that we know or can imagine. So closely attuned are they that one often knows what the other is thinking, so tied together that what hurts one hurts the other and what brings joy to one brings joy to the other also.

"I and the Father are one." There are those who take that in the first sense, who believe that Jesus and God are one and the same: that Jesus *is* God. I am not constrained to argue with them, but I do want to point out that this has never been the majority opinion, so to speak, in the church. And the reason it has not is that the New Testament, including this Gospel itself, uses so many other phrases that imply also some type of separation, some type of distinction. To call Jesus the "Son of God" is itself one such phrase. However similar and alike and identical in genes and chromosomes and will and purpose and idea a father and a son may be, there is yet a real and permanent difference between them also. We read that "no one has ever seen God" (John 1:18). We read that God has knowledge of which Jesus is ignorant (concerning the end of the age, for example, Mark 13:32.) We read that Jesus said that God was greater than he (John 15:28) and that God sent him (John 12:45). We read that God is the head of Christ as a husband is the head of his wife (I Cor. 11:3.) We read that a believer is "Christ's" as "Christ is God's" (I Cor. 3:23) or "in" Christ as Christ is "in" God, and vice versa (II Cor. 13:5; John 14:20.) We read that Jesus is "the image [in contemporary terms, "the model"] of the invisible God" (Col. 1:15), "the likeness of God" (II Cor. 4:4), that he "reflects the glory of God and bears the very stamp of his nature" (Heb. 1:3), and that "God was with him" (Acts 10:38).

So it is that the general consensus has always insisted that Jesus and God are one only in some sense that two separate persons can be one, a sense that I have tried to suggest by the analogy of marriage: "a mystical and spiritual" union, if you will—the closest conceivable connection, the most intimate and binding and meaningful and demanding relationship that we can imagine or describe. Translated into practical terms, what does the incarnation, the divinity of Christ, then mean?

It means, for one thing, that *every man has a divine potential*. "The spirit of man," we read in the Old Testament, "is the lamp of the LORD." (Prov. 20:27.) Every man has a divine element, a moral consciousness, a "light that enlightens" (John 1:9). Sometimes people talk about the divinity of Christ in such a way that they effectively divorce Jesus from our common humanity. The "divine" and the "human"—to hear them talk—are about like oil and water: they never mix or interpenetrate each other.

But the overwhelming witness of the New Testament is that the divinity of Jesus was a filling up, a completion, a perfection of his humanity. He "was like his brethren," we read, "in every respect" (Heb. 2:17). His physical life was human in every respect like our own: subject to growth, weariness, hunger, thirst, pleasure, suffering, death. His emotional apparatus was human in every respect. He was "tempted as we are" (Heb. 4:15). He was astonished, compassionate, indignant, disappointed by turn. He became so greatly distressed that he said, "My soul is very sorrowful, even to death" (Mark 14:34). His mental life was human in every respect. He learned obedience through suffering (Heb. 5:8). He grew not only in stature but also in wisdom; he learned by seeing and doing. His spiritual life was human in every respect. He prayed to God—sometimes in exaltation and sometimes in sorrow and even in agony with "loud cries and tears" (Heb. 5:7). He openly repudiated the notion that he was as good as God, and he equally clearly subordinated himself to the Holy Spirit when he said that a sin against himself could be forgiven, but not one against the Spirit. So he lived his life, did his work, bore his sorrows, faced his temptations without a single resource that is not available to every human being. His only equipment was his humanity. His divinity was his humanity raised to its highest power and therefore means that human nature has a divine potential.

There is a strange passage in the book of Genesis describing a primitive ritual (Gen. 15:7–21). Abram sacrificed some animals, cutting each in half and laying them opposite to one another. "When the sun had gone down and it was dark, behold, a smoking fire pot and a flaming torch passed between these pieces." What did it mean? The next verse goes on to say, "On that day the Lord made a covenant with Abram." It is a symbolic way of saying that there is an affinity between God and man, that they are two halves of the same whole, they can make agreements together. After all, a man cannot make a covenant—a legal contract—with an ant or a fish; nor can they with us. If there is to be a covenant between two parties, they must have complementary natures.

Jesus Christ—the revelation of what God is—is also the sign of what man may become. His divinity, the incarnation, means that human life has a capacity for the divine. As II Peter puts it, we can "become partakers of the divine nature" (II Peter 1:4).

Another thing this means is that *the Christian way of life is natural. It is normal.* It is the life for which we were intended. It is not something esoteric, foreign to our natures. It is not otherworldly or supernatural or against the grain, but supremely natural.

The conception was rampant in Jesus' time, and still persists into our own, that the natural is opposed to the divine and is therefore evil. When the ancients pictured the overthrow of evil they thought of cataclysmic events shaking the natural world. When they thought of God revealing himself they thought of unnatural events like burning bushes that were not consumed, earthshaking thunders, and virgin mothers. They thought that the Son of God would surely be a supernatural figure of dazzling might.

But it didn't happen that way. Jesus came—"a tiny baby thing, that made a woman cry." Or, as the beloved carol puts it:

> How silently, how silently
>   The wondrous gift is given!
> So God imparts to human hearts
>   The blessings of His heaven.
> No ear may hear His coming,
>   But in this world of sin,
> Where meek souls will receive Him still,
>   The dear Christ enters in.[39]

And when that baby was a mature man his divinity was so natural and unobtrusive that most folks never saw it at all!

The Christian life is the normal life; all others are aberrations and abnormalities. The Christian is the true man. We were not made for rebellion against God; we were made for fellowship with God. A man is true to his own nature only when he is true to Christ. There is a poem by Bonaro Overstreet which means more and more to me:

> Are not my hands my own?
>   How is it, then,
> That I stand here alone within my kitchen,
> Intent upon the making of a pie,
> And suddenly my mother's hands have slipped
> Inside of mine . . . and mine are only gloves
> Made flexible by what she wills to do
> With flour and salt and shortening?
>   I stare down:
> My hands, proved mine by permanent signature.
> And yet . . . their motions . . .
>   I have seen before
> Fingers that held a pie-plate in mid-air
> Upon their tips that spread to balance it;
> And I have seen a hand that slid a blade
> Around the pie plate, neatly shearing off
> Unwanted crust that dangled to the board
> To crumple there into a little heap.
> This is familiar. But it was not I
> Who poised the plate, or drew the cutting blade.
> That was my mother.[40]

The natural thing is for us to have that feeling of being gloves on God's hands. "It is no longer I who live," says Paul, "but Christ who lives in me." (Gal. 2:20.) God's Spirit so cooperates in silent and indiscernible ways with our own endeavors that we cannot distinguish between the influences of that Spirit and the natural faculties of our own minds.

Chapter 8

THE RIDDLE
OF RIGHTEOUSNESS

A STRANGE TRANSACTION has taken place three times since Israel has become a modern state. The orthodox rabbis of Israel have sold the whole country to an obliging Arab. The Arab gave the rabbis power of attorney, which enabled them to buy back the state a year later. It sounds as though there must have been some sort of tax angle, but there wasn't. The "angle" was this: The rabbis were avoiding breaking the old Levitical law (Lev. 25:3–4) which says that every seventh year the land of Israel shall lie fallow. The modern government of Israel and most of the citizens are far from being strict, religious Jews and they had no intention whatever of allowing everything to stand still for a year while weeds grew in the fields and fruit rotted on the trees. So the orthodox rabbis "sold" the country to a non-Jew, then bought it back when the sabbatical year was over, thus avoiding breaking the Biblical injunction.

Why did they do it? They did it because they thought it was the right thing to do; they did it as a way of obeying God. Keeping the Law with its 613 specific commands, even by such devious technicalities, is a solution to the perennial problem of all religious people. It is the problem you might call the riddle of righteousness, the question of how to know the right thing to do, how to know and follow God's will in everyday life.

This riddle, how to know and do the right thing, is crucial for every last one of us. In the long run, getting the right relationship with reality is decisive. In the natural world, those plants and animals which do not adjust to reality die. In the mental and emotional world the one who is, as the psychiatrists say, "disoriented from reality" needs help. At the very least, a mistake about reality condemns one to a life of futility, like a hen trying to hatch a glass egg! How to get right with reality is of interest to us all.

The apostle Paul was brought up under the Jewish law and his greatest contribution to Christianity is in his forging of a different answer to the riddle of righteousness. He had zealously done his best to keep the commandments. Like that other young man who came to Jesus, he could have said truthfully that he had observed them all from his youth up (Mark 10:20), but, also like that young man, he hadn't found thereby the abundant life. He had no peace of mind or poise of spirit until, through Christ, he found a new and different answer.

I

In the letter to the Romans, Paul gives the better answer that came to him. Romans is the longest and most important of his letters and was written in the full maturity of his life and thought. It has, really, just a single theme: *What God wants of us is faith.* The riddle of righteousness is not solved by keeping even a holy, just, and good law; it is not solved by disciplining one-self; it is not solved—as most Americans think—by being as good as the next fellow. It is solved only by faith. "The righteous," he says, "shall live by faith." (Rom. 1:17.)

And what does he mean by "faith"? Does he mean the intellectual acceptance of certain teachings? Does he mean accepting the incredible? Does he mean naïve acceptance of the unprovable? No. He means an inward discovery which enables a person to stand anything that can happen to him.

What is it that can do that? *What is the faith that saves us?* What is the discovery which enables a person to stand anything that can happen? *It is the confident conviction that God is good.* For Paul, faith is an all-out attitude of confidence in God's goodness; it is a conscious-ness that unreservedly trusts itself to that goodness; it is as absolute and as rewarding a dependence upon God as that of a child on a wise and generous and loving father. This is what really got through to Paul that day near Damascus; by vicarious identification with Jesus he began to act from love, like a son, rather than from hope of gain, like a slave. We all know the difference in attitude between a son who does things for his father out of love and respect and admiration and an employee who does things for pay or out of fear that he will lose his job or out of hope of a promotion. They may do the same things, but they do them from a different motive. And that inner spirit subtly but surely affects the quality of the work. To change the analogy, there is a world of difference between a doctor who always wanted to be a doctor and one who calculatingly chose it because it promised a good income. They do the same things but from different motives, and we can feel a difference in their work. So an attitude of faith, as compared to an attitude of legal obedience, affects the religious result.

"But," someone may be saying to himself, "how do we know that God is good?" As a character in a novel says, "Where we had thought a god, somehow akin to ourselves, ruled in the universe, it may be there is nothing but black emptiness and a coldness worse than cruelty." Remember that line from Ecclesiastes: "The righteous and the wise . . . are in the hand of God; whether it is love or hate man does not know" (Eccl. 9:1)? How can we be confident that God is good?

There are two reasons. One is that we know how good Jesus was, and surely the Father is as good as the Son! We know that Jesus forgave even those who crucified him; we know that he understood the sick and the sinners whom society had cast out; we know that he returned good for evil. Now, either that loving compassion was an accident or it was a revelation. And down through the years more and more people have concluded that the New Testament authors were right—that Jesus is a revelation of what God is like.

The other reason we know that God is good is by our own personal experience. I am growing more and more to doubt if anyone ever becomes more than a superficial Christian without some personal experience that convinces him that God has been good to him far beyond his deserving. Phillips Brooks says his parents were so poor that his mother once exclaimed "that for her own part she expected to die in the poor house." "At that," says the great preacher, "father dropped his hands to the table, and his eyes sparkled, and he said, 'My dear, I have trusted God for forty years, and he never has forsaken me; I am not going to distrust him now.'" That struck home to his son. "It was better than the catechism," Brooks says. "It sank into me; and during my earlier life I went through perils of sickness and poverty and all forms of limitation and trouble, but I never lost sight of that scene and that sentence." It was a personal experience with an eternal value for him. The faith that enables us to stand anything is the conviction that God is good.

A second question to be raised is this: *From what does this faith save us?* Paul's answer is that it saves us from self-righteousness. It saves us from the proud idea that we are just about all right as we are. Once a man gets a real purchase on the outgoing goodness of God, he realizes how inadequate he himself is. "I bid every one among you not to think of himself more highly than he ought to think," says Paul. (Rom. 12:3.)

Every good man knows he is not good enough to be worth saving. If you will step back from yourself a minute, you will see what I mean. Can you number the times you have deliberately disobeyed or stifled the voice of conscience? Can you number the times you fudged a little here or cheated a little there? Are you the person God had a right to expect you to be? I suppose there have been few lives in the twentieth century of more saintly quality than that of Mahatma Gandhi. But what does he think of himself? He quotes four lines:

> Where is there a wretch
> So wicked and loathsome as I?
> I have forsaken my Maker,
> So faithless have I been.[41]

If this good man thought that, where do we stand?

A preacher was once exhorting a group of skid road derelicts. Our native American confidence in ourselves and our own abilities was running at just about full tide then, and this preacher was using Kipling's poem "If" as the theme of his sermon. By way of conclusion he recited the whole thing in round, unctious tones, pausing dramatically after that next-to-last line:

> If you can fill the unforgiving minute
> With sixty seconds' worth of distance run . . .[42]

In the perfect hush a voice from the rear was heard to ask, "What if you can't?" Just so! What if you can't! What if we can't control the H-bomb? What if we can't throw out this devil of racism from our country? What if we can't stop this fratricidal escalation in the Middle East? What if you can't stop your drinking? What if you can't make your homelife happy? What if you can't live up to your ideals? There is no salvation for us until we know that we are not self-sufficient. There is no salvation for us until we know we cannot do what must be done without the help of a good God. What is it that faith saves us from? It saves us from the delusion of our own self-sufficiency, from thinking that we're just about all right as we are, from complacent self-satisfaction.

Still another question to be raised is this: *For what does this faith save us?* The answer, which is all too often lightly overlooked by those who study the letter to the Romans, is that *it saves us for lives of moral achievement.* It saves us for the business of forging characters molded on the Sermon on the Mount. It saves us that we may learn to overcome evil with good, to love our neighbors as ourselves, to conduct ourselves "not in reveling and drunkenness, not in debauchery and licentiousness, not in quarreling and jealousy," not in proud self-satisfaction, but in humility and "righteousness and peace and joy."

Some people's thinking about the Christian life seems

to be that it consists in being forgiven one's sins. Others cannot see the equity in a system that would allow a man to live fast and loose, then repent on his deathbed and be saved. The point that both miss is that canceling the past does not make a record of achievement. It leaves the past a wasteland and the future a blank. God's forgiveness may erase our guilt, but only moral effort can make spiritual character grow and develop as it should. "You will know them by their fruits," says the Master. "Not every one who says to me, 'Lord, Lord,' shall enter the kingdom of heaven, but he who does the will of my Father." Moral obedience is the only test of discipleship. Moral achievement, Christlike character, is the badge of our faithfulness.

There is no better illustration of what the letter to the Romans is all about than the life of John Wesley. As a young priest in the Church of England he was desperately and determinedly bent on proving his place among the elect. But the more he fasted and prayed and took Communion and read his Bible and visited the poor, the less certain he was of himself. Then, under the influence of Paul's understanding of faith he began to sense the goodness of God in a powerful way. His preaching changed and became so persuasive that habitual drunkards became temperate, whoremongers fled their fornication, thieves became honest, and those who had cursed with every breath learned to love and serve the Lord. According to Lecky, the English historian, Wesley's religious revolution was of greater importance to England than all the splendid military and political battles won by Prime Minister Pitt. Not merely hundreds, nor even thousands, but millions of lives were changed for the better because a man named Wesley had passed their way.

II

There is one Biblical text which I think of on the golf course more often than any other. "I do not understand my own actions," writes Paul. "For I do not do what I want, but I do the very thing I hate. . . . I can will what is right, but I cannot do it" (Rom. 7:15, 18). I can will a drive straight as a string with just enough hook on it to get a good roll or a slight fade—as the case may require—for good control, but I cannot do it! There is almost always a gap between my desires, or my intentions, and my performance.

So with most of us. There is a gap between what we mean to do in raising a family and what we actually do; there is a gap between the way we mean to drive a car and the way we really do it; there is almost always a gap between what we intend or desire as students or businessmen or whatever and what we really accomplish. And the same thing is true, of course, in the religious and moral and ethical realm—there is almost always a gap between our intention and our performance.

Paul attributes this difference to forces he feels struggling within himself, forces that he calls "law" and "sin" and "flesh" and "mind." Well, it doesn't much matter whether you put those labels on them or the psychoanalyst's "id," "ego," and "superego," or the labels of something else. Everyone knows what it is to feel the pull of conflicting inner forces:

Within my earthly temple there's a crowd;
There's one of us that's humble, one that's proud,
There's one that's broken-hearted for his sins,
There's one that unrepentant sits and grins;

There's one that loves his neighbor as himself,
And one that cares for nought but fame and pelf.
From much corroding care I should be free
If I could once determine which is me.[43]

Carl Rogers, a leading authority in the counseling and interpersonal relationships field, wrote sometime ago:

> In my work at the Counseling Center of the University of Chicago, I have the opportunity of working with people who present a wide variety of personal problems. There is the student concerned about failing in college; the housewife disturbed about her marriage; the responsible professional man who . . . functions inefficiently in his work; . . . the parent who is distressed by his child's behavior; the popular girl who finds herself unaccountably overtaken by sharp spells of black depression; the woman who fears that life and love are passing her by. . . . I have, however, come to believe that in spite of this bewildering horizontal multiplicity, and the layer upon layer of vertical complexity . . . that at bottom each person is asking, "Who am I, *really?* How can I get in touch with this real self, underlying all my surface behavior?" [44]

So the counselor says what the poet said and Paul before him: "From much corroding care I should be free/If I could once determine which is me." "I do not understand my own actions. . . . I can will what is right, but I cannot do it."

Paul points out that in this struggle, God is working for good. The goal of all God's activity appears to be the creation of responsible, free, loving persons. And even in the fiercest of these inner stormy conflicts, he says God is working toward that end: "We know that in everything God works for good" (Rom. 8:28).

One of the pioneers who have helped to bring together the insights of profound and creative religion with those of clinical psychology is Anton Boisen. His personal experience was devastating—it shattered him mentally and emotionally not once but several times. In looking back over a long and influential life of helping the mentally ill, he had this to say:

> I believe that certain forms of mental illness, particularly those characterized by anxiety and conviction of sin, are not evils. They are instead manifestations of the power that makes for health. They are analogous to fever or inflammation in the body. I am thus very sure that the experience which plunged me into this new field of labor was mental illness of the most profound and unmistakable variety. . . . A review of this record will show that I have passed through five psychotic episodes. . . . Severe though they were, they have been for me problem-solving experiences. They have left me not worse but better.[45]

This is one thing, then, to remember about our inner conflicts: God is working in and through them for good.

Let us move on to note another of Paul's insights: *God's work is of little or no avail to those who do not love him, who are not responsive to his lead.* "We know that in everything God works for good," he says. But without stopping for breath, he continues, "with those who love him, who are called according to his purpose" (Rom. 8:28). Although God is continually at work through our inner turmoils and shocks and uncertainties, his work is of little practical avail if we are not responsive to him. He causes the rain to fall on all, but only the farmer who cooperates with it reaps a crop of any value.

Every now and again, when I am called to the home of someone who has undergone a great strain or shock, I am told that the family have been trying to pray "but can't seem to get through." They don't have any awareness that God is listening or caring; they feel cut off and isolated. I do not tell them this, but the fact is that almost invariably that in itself is a result of lives that have been pretty self-centered. Except for some purely formal or perfunctory gestures, they have left God out of their lives. He has been as remote from their conscious choices and daily activities as the stars in their courses are from one's decision to have a second helping of potatoes and gravy.

"It takes two to tango," and there are also other experiences that it takes two to complete. Once there was a little boy who was playing hide-and-seek with another youngster. He hid himself and waited for his playmate to come. He waited for a long time, but no one came. Finally he came out, to discover that the other was nowhere to be seen. In fact, he realized, the other little boy had not been looking for him at all. With tears brimming in his eyes, he ran to his father, sobbing, "I hide, but no one wants to seek me." So with this, despite all God's work for good, the experience is not completed unless we do our part, unless we love him and respond to his purpose.

A blind person was learning to walk by faith rather than by sight at a training center for Seeing Eye dogs. As the learner, dog, and instructor crossed a street, the teacher said: "Walk closer to him. He cannot guide you if you hold him at arm's length." So this passage speaks to us: God's work for our good is of little avail to those who do not love him, who hold him at arm's length, who are not responsive to his lead.

Let us look at one more thing that Paul says: *no inner turmoil or outside force need separate us from God's love.*

> Who shall separate us from the love of Christ? Shall tribulation, or distress, or persecution, or famine, or nakedness, or peril, or sword? . . . No, in all these things we are more than conquerors. . . . Neither death, nor life, . . . nor anything else in all creation, will be able to separate us from the love of God. (Rom. 8:35 ff.)

Woodrow Wilson was a highly strung person and never robust physically. He couldn't even complete his university studies because his health broke down. Not long after, he discouragedly wrote to a friend, "How can a man with a weak body ever arrive anywhere?" He finished his law studies privately, however, and finally was admitted to practice. Not long after that he met, furiously courted, and married Ellen Axson. This is what he once wrote to her: "You are the only person in the world with whom I do not have to act a part. To whom I do not have to deal out confidences cautiously. . . . My salvation is in being loved." So with us all. Our salvation is in being loved, and no inner turmoil or outer circumstance need separate us from God's love.

Does that sound a little too idealistic or a little too sentimental to you? No one, I trust, will hurl those charges against the Green Bay Packers who in the middle sixties were in pro football what the New York Yankees used to be in baseball, or the Boston Celtics were in basketball. After one of their Super Bowl games an interviewer asked Coach Vince Lombardi how the Packers were able to come up with so many great plays in the clutch. Lombardi was not a soft and sloppy man; (one of his players once said that he played football for three reasons: (a) the love of the game, (b) the money, and (c) the fear of Lombardi); he was on coast-to-coast television and knew full well that anything he said could be used against him. What did he say? He said, "Because they have respect for one another. . . . They have a great deal of love for one another." And another pro player, commenting on that remark, said that a pro team has to run on love.

> You go through so much together. There's the physical torture . . . you watch your teammates get hurt, cut, broken. You watch them lose their jobs, you watch them go to the heights of victory together and the depths of despair together. You share every conceivable emotion . . . and pretty soon your life is intimately bound up in theirs, and this intense love and devotion springs up.
> It's funny: after a win you have the greatest feeling in the world, but the week after you lose a ball game you walk down the street and you feel like you don't have any friends and the writers are climbing on you and the sportscasters are jumping you and the people don't want your autograph. So where do you turn? You turn to the 40 guys that are still in there working and suffering with you; you can always depend on them.[46]

Our salvation is in being loved, and the good news is that there is nothing which need separate us from God's love.

Chapter 9

THE GREATEST THINGS
IN THE WORLD

It's AN ILL WIND that blows no good. There was once a church split into factions over who was the best preacher it had ever had. Some members of that church had fallen into moral difficulties, others were being accused of false worship, and still others were suing one another in the courts. As though all this wasn't enough, there was also a fanatical fringe that was trying to turn every meeting into an emotional orgy, and there were some who were using the Lord's Supper as a time to get drunk. To cap it all, some of the eggheads were busy denying the church's teaching on immortality.

It is, however, an ill wind that blows *no* good. Were it not for this church and its troubles we would never have had what we now call The First Letter of Paul to the Corinthians. Were it not for their factionalism we would not have the ringing question, "Is Christ divided?" (I Cor. 1:13), nor the matchless description of the work of the ministry: "Paul . . . planted, Apollos watered, but God gave the growth. So neither he who plants nor he who waters is anything, but only God who gives the growth" (I Cor. 3:5–7). Were it not for the immorality of some, we might never have had the noblest estimate ever put on our physical selves: "Your body is a temple of the Holy Spirit" (I Cor. 6:19). Were it not for the skeptical, we would never have heard "the first clear treatment of the Christian's reasoned hope in victory over death" (the fifteenth chapter). And were it not for the fanatical fringe, who were mouthing gibberish, we would never have had one of the most familiar and beloved of all Biblical passages, the chapter on love (the thirteenth).

The situation was this: Paul had founded the church, but had moved on and was now in Ephesus. From time to time he heard how things were going at Corinth and wrote to the people to help them with their problems. He wrote at least four letters at different times and in different moods. One was written to answer questions that had been put to him and to urge the people to correct some abuses he had heard about via the grapevine. It is a letter of interest to every person who has ever been caught in, or wondered about, the internal problems of a church.

One of the problems in Corinth was with a few people who were going off the deep end emotionally. As such people often do, they were trying to make their own behavior the standard and norm for all. They were "speaking in tongues"—an ecstatic mouthing of incoherent syllables surging up from obscure emotional depths. Every now and again, in the history of the church, including this century, there is an outbreak of the same sort of thing. Paul speaks directly and plainly. He does not forbid speaking in tongues, but he very pointedly characterizes it as the lowest and least of the gifts of the Holy Spirit and urges the seeking of the higher gifts. And the greatest of all the gifts of the Spirit, he says, is Christlike love. Not love in any romantic or sentimental or self-centered sense, but "undiscourageable goodwill," a quality of ethical concern for the well-being of the whole being of everyone. Such love, he says, is the greatest thing in the world. Let us look at some of the reasons that is so.

I

Love is the greatest thing in the world because *it is indispensable*. Humanity cannot live without it; it is a necessity of our kind. Though one can speak in the tongues of men and of angels, without love he is worthless. Without love, knowledge and faith and philanthropy are sterile. Humanity cannot live without love.

It is clear that love is essential to healthy and normal personal existence. Humanity, among other things, is vulnerable to neuroticism. A neurotic is a person who is emotionally sick, a person who cannot seem to be happy even in fortunate circumstances, a person who cannot seem to face his share of life's problems. What makes people neurotic? Most neuroses seem to have at their root a conflict due to lack of love; neurotics all seem to have an unwanted feeling. In other words, human life, if it is to develop normally, must have love.

Moreover, we cannot function effectively without love, either. Would it be possible to be a housewife without love? Could one endure the spilled milk, the never-ending piles of dishes, the dirty laundry and the hot ironing, the insistent, piercing voices of youngsters, without love? Dr. A. B. Davidson used to comment on that well-known passage from Isaiah which says that they who wait upon the Lord "shall mount up with wings like eagles, they shall run and not be weary, they shall walk and not faint" (Isa. 40:31). He would say that most any of us mount up with wings like eagles, occasionally, in the inspiration of some great moment. And to run and not be weary is not such an unusual feat, either. A furious burst of energy sometimes amazes us with our own potentialities. But to walk and not faint is the most difficult of all things to accomplish. To keep at the daily round at a steady pace takes all that most of us have. And without love for family, or friends, or even for the job—without love we soon faint.

What is true of us as individuals holds for society also. No community can be healthily normal and effective if love is absent. Friendship disintegrates the moment that people begin to think exclusively of their own welfare instead of displaying concern for one another. Several people may live in the same house, but it is not a home unless they affectionately prefer one another. No material assets can cover a lack of goodwill. "Better a dinner of herbs where love is," opines the book of Proverbs, "than a fatted ox and hatred with it." (Prov. 15:17). So it is with every social unit right up to the nation and international affairs. When love—concerned, undiscourageable goodwill—goes, healthy social life goes with it.

Almost the last place on earth one would expect to find any support for the Christian view of life is in Bertrand Russell, the British philosopher. All his long life he stood for a nonreligious and nontheistic point of view. A few years ago, however, this Nobel Prize winner was in this country for a series of lectures at Columbia University. This is what he said: "The root of the matter (if we want a stable world) is a very simple and old-fashioned thing, a thing so simple that I am almost ashamed to mention it, for fear of the derisive smile with which wise cynics will greet my words. The thing I mean is love, Christian love, or compassion. If you feel this you have a motive for existence, a guide in action, a reason for courage, an imperative necessity for intellectual honesty." [47] Love is the greatest thing in the world because neither personal nor social health is possible without it.

Love, moreover, is the greatest thing in the world because *it is comprehensive of all other virtues.* "Love," says Paul, "is patient and kind; love is not jealous or boastful; it is not arrogant or rude. Love does not insist on its own way; it is not irritable or resentful; it does not rejoice at wrong, but rejoices in the right. Love bears all things, believes all things, hopes all things, endures all things." Or, as he puts it in another place, "Love is the fulfilling of the law" (Rom. 13:10).

The Jews of Jesus' and Paul's day were trying to work their way to heaven by keeping the Ten Commandments and a multitude of other commandments they had added to them. Jesus' whole life was a demonstration of a simpler way of doing God's will. Just do this one thing and the rest will take care of itself. If you love, you cannot help fulfill the whole law. What is the first of the Ten Commandments? "You shall have no other gods before me." If a person loves God, he will not have to be told that. Love is the fulfilling of that law. If a man loves his family, will you have to tell him to honor his father and his mother? If one loves his neighbor as himself, will you have to tell him not to murder or not to steal or not to covet? Love is the fulfilling of all these commandments. Love is comprehensive of all other virtues.

A. J. Cronin in *Adventures in Two Worlds* told of an incident that happened in Connecticut. Henry Adams was just an average white-collar worker who took an average pride in his modest home and garden, his wife, and his three children—two girls and a boy. The boy was his assistant in the garden, and many a happy hour they had together. When the war came the Adamses decided to take in a refugee child for the duration. Henry wasn't too wild about the idea, but he agreed. So a little Central European by the name of Paul Pietrostanalsi came to live with them.

The boy was half starved, bony, with close-cropped hair and frightened eyes and could not speak a word of English. But Adams took an immediate liking to him.

As the weeks slipped past, the Adamses began to taste disillusionment. Perhaps because of the terrors of war and privation and uprooting Paul was hard to handle. He had confused ideas about honesty and obedience. As he acquired English he turned out to be adept at stretching the truth in convenient ways. He was withdrawn and evasive. Toward the girls in the family he was neutral, and he merely tolerated his foster parents. His only attachment was to the young boy, Sammy.

One day Paul had a sore throat. Against strict instructions, he had gone swimming in a creek known to be polluted. His fever rose, and since the danger of contagion was great, he had to be isolated in his room and none of the children, not even his beloved Sammy, could see him. Then one morning when Henry Adams went in to wake Sammy he found that Paul had crept from his room to Sammy's and had gotten into bed with his sleeping chum. Now he was sleeping with his face next to that of Sammy. A week later Sammy was dead from the virulent infection.

Sometime later Cronin paid a visit to the Adamses. To his surprise Paul was helping Henry in the garden. "You still have him?" Cronin questioned. "Yes, and he's improved quite a bit. They're giving him some gland tablets. He's quieter and brighter. And," added Henry

with a quiet smile, "you won't have any trouble pronouncing his last name anymore. He's Paul Adams now.
You see, we've adopted him." [48] Love is the greatest thing
in the world, because it is comprehensive of all the virtues.

Love is the greatest thing in the world, once more,
because *the capacity to love has no boundaries and no
limitations.* It is not limited by time, "love never ends"
(I Cor. 13:8). It is not limited by quantity, nobody ever
feels that he can either love or be loved too much. Each
child in a family of ten can have as much love from his
mother as an only child. Love is not limited by our
physical endowment. We know in part and we prophesy
in part, but one mentally retarded can love as fully as a
genius. Someone has suggested an analogy for the power
of God. The capacity of a water or electrical system is
always limited, he pointed out. Only so many can be
connected before the pressure or the voltage drops. But
there is no limit to the number of television or radio
aerials you can put up to tune in on the same station.
The power of God, he said, is like that. So is his love.
And love is the way we can be most like him. "God is
love," says the New Testament, "and he who abides in
love abides in God, and God abides in him." (I John
4:16).

During the bus boycott in Montgomery, Alabama,
Martin Luther King's house was bombed. He was at a
meeting, but his wife and baby and a friend were home.
By the time he got home a crowd had gathered, and
city officials and newspaper reporters were on hand. The
mayor had officially proclaimed a "get tough" policy, and
the white policemen were doing their best to put it into
effect. But the crowd did not disperse, and its mood got
uglier and uglier, until the city officials and white re-

porters in the house began to worry about whether they would ever get out unharmed. Then King went out to speak to the crowd. He told the people that no one had been injured. Then he told them not to get panicky, and urged them to take home any weapons they might have. "We cannot solve this problem through . . . violence," he said. "We must meet violence with nonviolence. Remember the words of Jesus: 'He who lives by the sword will perish by the sword.'" And he ended with this, "We must love our white brothers no matter what they do to us. We must make them know that we love them. . . . 'Love your enemies; bless them that curse you; pray for them that despitefully use you.' This is what we must live by. We must meet hate with love." [49] The crowd's mood changed, and the people eventually dispersed peacefully. Martin Luther King had a hold on something there that nothing can stop! Neither brutality nor tribulation nor courtrooms nor peril nor famine nor political powers nor death itself can stop love.

II

Memorial Day has been a formal part of our national life for almost a hundred years, but it stems from a human impulse much older and deeper. From time immemorial, I suppose, people have set aside certain times for remembering their dead; and for something over fifteen hundred years Christians have set aside a day—sometimes in May, more usually now in November—as All Saints' Day, a time to remember all the faithful and bring to mind the battles they fought, the defeats they endured, the victories they won over temptations and obstacles and discouragements of every kind. There is probably not one of us for whom such an occasion does not personally recall someone whom he will never forget. Your father or mother, your husband or wife, your brother or sister, your child, your friend, or your hero: you will never forget them no matter how long you live and no matter what happens to you.

The question that almost inevitably comes to mind, of course, is: What has happened to them? Have "they become as though they had not been born" (Sirach 44:9)? Have their lives, whether long or short, guttered out or been snuffed out like a candle flame? While we may personally remember them during our lifetimes, is all their meaning and value and existence finally nothing more than a vanishing footprint on the sands of time? Or are they gone, as a poet put it three hundred years ago, "into the world of light"—to some other and better life? How much stock are we to put in the Biblical confidence that we are "surrounded" by a "great cloud of witnesses" (Heb. 12:1), or the ancient affirmations that we "believe . . . in the communion of saints," "the resurrection of the dead, and the life of the world to come"?

Our subject now is literally a matter of life and death. Is there any real sense in remembering those who have fought in our nation's wars if all they were was just cannon fodder rubbed out in the course of the rise and fall of one more earthly civilization that will have its day and cease to be? Does it make any difference whether what you do (or have done) as a parent has any real, permanent, abiding possibilities or whether it ultimately all goes for nothing anyhow? Even the youth have a stake in knowing whether discipline and education and effort pay off finally or whether it would not be smarter to "eat, drink, and be merry," for on some tomorrow it will all end finally and completely anyhow.

The earliest and clearest Christian thinking on the

subject of immortality (or resurrection, or eternal life—for our purpose here they are synonyms) is in the fifteenth chapter of First Corinthians.

Paul here maintains that *our belief in immortality fits nature and human nature as we know them.* It is in accord with what we think we know about the universe. Look at a grain of wheat, he says. It never reaches its ultimate potential until it is planted in the ground and "dies"—that is, until the grain itself actually disappears, until its form is completely changed. If you were to dig up a growing stalk of wheat, you would never find anything at its root that even faintly resembles the grain of wheat which was planted. So also, he argues, is immortality—our immortal selves don't look any more like our mortal selves than the roots look like the seed. Look at the bodies of birds and animals, he says. They don't look alike, yet all fulfill the necessary functions of bodies. So why must our immortal means of communication—which is what a body is—look like our mortal ones? Our immortal bodies are to our mortal ones as the butterfly is to the caterpillar. The sun and the moon and the stars all look quite different from one another, yet all give light to the earth. In short, Paul says that what Christians believe about being given a spiritual body to supersede the physical body fits what we see in the natural world around us.

Furthermore, he goes on, the idea of immortality fits what we know (or think we know) about human nature. Naturally his idea of the origin and nature of man was based on the prescientific world view of the book of Genesis, and his method of Biblical study was that of the Jewish rabbis; doubtless his psychology was primitive and the scholarly tools at his command were limited. Yet, what he had learned in the best schools of his time, when added to his own observation of the way he and others acted, fitted the idea of immortality. "Just as we have borne the image of the man of dust, we shall also bear the image of the man of heaven." (I Cor. 15:49.)

That general proposition still holds. Belief in immortality fits what we know, or think we know, about nature and human nature. Advances in knowledge in geology or biology or zoology or psychology or sociology have not made belief in immortality irrational or obsolete. Some scientists, of course, do not believe in it, but others do; and science is powerless to render a final verdict. The more we know, the greater the number of unknown possibilities that open before us. All that any of us can do is to frame a hypothesis that seems to cover all the known facts; and for many, the most reasonable hypothesis is one that includes immortality. As Wernher von Braun, the missileman, put it a while ago, "I believe in an immortal soul." Why? Because much scientific thinking currently holds to the theory of the conservation of energy—that matter is just congealed energy, as it were, and can never be destroyed but only changed in form. In short, that the universe conserves its physical values. To him, therefore, it is not out of line to believe that the universe also conserves its moral and spiritual values: "Life and soul . . . cannot disintegrate into nothingness, and so are immortal."

And psychology, the science of human nature, is at least equally compatible with belief in immortality. We learn more every day about the interaction of our bodies and our personalities, and all medicine is to some degree psychosomatic medicine. The brain appears more and more to be like a computer—good at scanning and feedback and memory, but essentially controlled by some sort of programmer: the ego or the psyche or the soul or the personality. The belief in immortality fits what we know about nature and human nature at least as well as it did in Paul's time.

A second important thing Paul says in this chapter is this: *immortality conserves character values.* If there is no immortality, where was the gain in his being courageous enough to speak out fearlessly even when it meant being thrown to the wild beasts in the arena at Ephesus (I Cor. 15:32)? Where is the sense of morality and integrity and discipline and effort? "If the dead are not raised," to quote him exactly, " 'Let us eat and drink, for tomorrow we die' " (I Cor. 15:32). This immortality which seems to fit so well what we know about the world around us and about our own natures must primarily be a conserver of character values—of love and honesty and integrity and generosity and kindness and self-control.

Character values are conserved. Someone once told about a retired British officer who had returned from service in India to his native England. Once, after recounting to friends some of his experiences, he said, "I expect to see something more thrilling than anything I have seen yet." His hearers were surprised, for he was more than seventy years old and had lived a full life and was retired from active service! What was he talking about? In a subdued tone he said, "I mean the first five minutes after death." No doubt it will be thrilling in the sense of being new and novel! But there is little reason to suppose that it will be remarkable in terms of what we will be. Here is a man who is generous, just, kind. Five minutes after death he will still be generous, just, kind. Here is a man who is selfish, narrow, conceited. Five minutes after death he is still going to be selfish, narrow, conceited. Death is not some magical process by which sinners are metamorphosed into saints; if we are cheap and superficial now, we will be cheap and superficial then. It is a birth into a new kind of life, and it does not change the nature of our character any more drastically than a baby is changed by birth from the fetus it was five minutes before birth.

Still another important thing Paul says is that *immortality is conditional*. All those who are like Adam die, he says, while all those who are like Christ live (cf. I Cor. 15:48). If you choose to live for earthly values, as the ancient story of Adam and Eve so dramatically puts them, then you haven't got the kind of character values that immortality preserves. "As was the man of dust, so are those who are of the dust." But if you choose to live for spiritual values, if you lay up treasures in heaven, as the Master put it, if you strive to be like Jesus, then you've got the kind of character values that immortality preserves. "As is the man of heaven, so are those who are of heaven." It depends on our being Christlike.

Al Smith, toward the close of his days, was an executive of the then newly built Empire State Building in New York City. He enjoyed showing friends and visitors the marvels of the skyscraper. One day while leading a group he had to cope with a woman who continually asked irrelevant questions. He tried his best to answer them patiently, but as the end of the tour drew near the last straw came. While going down in the elevator, the lady asked, "Suppose the elevator cables should break, would we go up or down?" "That, madam," the ex-governor replied, "depends entirely upon the kind of life you've been leading." Al Smith was hardly a theologian, but that is the authentic New Testament point of view! The future life is morally conditioned. "Not everyone who says to me, 'Lord, Lord,' " says Jesus, is going to inherit the Kingdom. Not everyone who mouths a prayer when he's in a jam, or who keeps up a sentimental acquaintance with religion, is going to be fit to live in the Kingdom. Does anyone suppose that he can thumb his nose at God by living an uninterruptedly self-centered life and then suddenly find himself at home in the house of many mansions?

Almost everyone knows something of the story of Anne Sullivan and Helen Keller. When the brilliant and devoted teacher who had been ears and eyes to Miss Keller for almost fifty years died, Miss Keller wrote in her diary that it was as though she herself had been cut in two. Nevertheless, she had promised to make a trip to Japan in the interest of promoting educational opportunities for the blind, and in a few months she was on her way. On one of the last days at sea, she wrote this: "And as I stood on the deck this morning in the midst of dawn, looking westward to the land where a great adventure awaits me, I thought I could feel her by my side." Did she or didn't she? Was this fantasy or fact? Was it a trick of her mind, or an intuitive grasp of something real? Was she the victim of an illusion or the witness of an invisible reality? I cannot answer for you. But this much is sure. If there is no immortality, it is not the mean and the narrow and the grasping souls of this earth who have been deceived. It is the high and the holy, the noble and the great—in ancient times people like Socrates, Plato, Cicero, Jesus, Paul; and in more modern times Descartes, Kant, Goethe, Darwin, Lincoln, Helen Keller, Albert Schweitzer! "Therefore . . . be steadfast, immovable, always abounding in the work of the Lord, knowing that in the Lord your labor is not in vain." (I Cor. 15:58.)

III

A year or two ago a documentary picture, in color, was released by the Atomic Energy Commission. It was the story of the scientific effort that reached a decisive turning point on December 2, 1942, in the metallurgical laboratory at the University of Chicago when the first sustained nuclear chain reaction was achieved; and it was called *The Day Tomorrow Began*.

No one will doubt the propriety of that title. The unlocking of nuclear energy was in truth the opening of a new era in human life and affairs. Neither war nor peace can ever be the same again; sustained nuclear fission has changed weapons and medicine and the temperature of our rivers; it has put new words in our vocabulary and strontium 90 in our bones.

Of course neither Einstein nor Fermi nor Oppenheimer nor Teller really invented anything new; they simply discovered something that had been true all along. "The day tomorrow began" is a graphic way of saying that we suddenly saw, in a new and decisive way, something that had always been true about atomic particles and structures. So one might equally say that the day Columbus discovered America was a day that tomorrow began. Or, again, that moment when Neil Armstrong took that one small step onto the moon, which was also a "giant leap for mankind," was a day tomorrow began.

Easter is the day tomorrow began for us religiously, the day we suddenly saw in a new and decisive way something that had always been true. Easter, as one of the New Testament writers put it, is the day that "life and immortality were brought to light" (II Tim. 1:10). It is not something invented by or for Jesus—any more than Einstein made atoms fissionable; it is something that was revealed by God through him. As Paul puts it, "If there is no resurrection of the dead, then Christ has not been raised" (I Cor. 15:13). His resurrection was dependent upon a general truth, not the other way around.

But upon what does that general truth depend? It depends upon the nature of things, the kind of universe this is. Columbus' trip depended upon the earth's being more or less round; nuclear fission and moon landings depend upon this being an ordered and dependable universe in which "energy equals mass times the square of the speed of light" yesterday, today, and forever. So with immortality; it depends upon the kind of universe this is—whether it is a randomly self-assembled and mindlessly operating electrochemical servomechanism of some sort, or whether it is the expression of goodness and love. It is that which makes the crucial difference when you are so sick that your life hangs in the balance, or so lonely that grief is your only companion, or you have dreamed a great dream only to have picayune realities steal it from you!

I invite you to look now at one of the most famous and helpful and beloved ways that this nature of things has ever been described: the Twenty-third Psalm. It is not from Paul's pen, of course. It is from an unknown genius of Old Testament times. But it is echoed in and worthy of the New Testament and can be helpful to Christians beyond measure.

What this man had learned about the heart of things he put in a figure of speech: "The Lord is my shepherd." That figure, perhaps, isn't as communicative in our time as it was in his; there may be persons reading this who have never seen a real live shepherd.

The psalmist begins with life's pleasant places:

> The Lord is my shepherd, I shall not want;
>> he makes me lie down in green pastures.
> He leads me beside still waters;
>> he restores my soul.
> He leads me the right way.

What does a sheep need? It needs food, pasture, grass. It needs rest, not only at night, but also to chew its cud. It needs water, and, shepherds say that not any little rushing streamlet will do, a sheep being the skittish creature it is; it must have a quiet pool or it will not drink, and in an arid country it must be led to these things.

And what do we need? Food, rest, water (it is amazing to most of us how quickly a man can die without water, as the late Bishop Pike did). These things are more than physical necessities; they are also the foundation of emotional stability and spiritual security; quietness and rest do actually and literally restore our souls.

Have we not been led in such pleasant places? There was a letter not long ago in Ann Landers' newspaper column, a letter of polite rebuke to millions of people who complain about their petty little ordinary problems. "Happiness," it said,

> is not getting that telegram: "We regret to inform you that your son was killed in action." Happiness is not getting a laboratory report which reads, "malignant." Happiness is not hearing the words . . . "your baby didn't live." Happiness is not receiving a phone call after midnight saying, "This is . . . the emergency hospital. Your daughter was in a serious accident." [50]

That does help keep things in perspective, doesn't it? That we have lacked nothing essential and enjoyed so much that is rewarding is the Lord's doing at least as much as our own, and it ought to be marvelous in our eyes.

The psalmist continues. He has recognized God's leading not only in the pleasant places of life but *also in the dark and dangerous places.*

> Even though I walk through a valley dark as death,
>   I fear no evil
> for you are with me;
>   your rod and your staff
>   strengthen me.

I don't know if they run sheep on the Steens Mountain in southeastern Oregon anymore, but they used to. It is almost the same height as Mt. Hermon in the Holy Land, and the general climate and surrounding topography are much the same. It has lots of little canyons, gorges, creeks, and gullies made by water and glaciation, and it is up such defiles that the shepherds take the sheep to summer range. On the east side of the mountain the bottoms of those gullies get pretty dark early in the afternoon, shaded by the mountain itself and by their own vegetation. Sheep, like every other living thing, have natural enemies which tend to take advantage of natural cover; those defiles, to a sheep, are literally as dark as death. But the shepherd knows that as well as the sheep, and in Biblical times he was prepared to beat off attackers with a heavy, primitive club something like a homemade mace and to rescue a sheep which had fallen, with the hooked end of his staff.

> You prepare a table before me
>   in the presence of my enemies;
> you anoint my head with oil,
>   my cup overflows.

Most commentators think the figure changes here from that of a shepherd to that of a human host. I do not. The shepherd is, in effect, host to his sheep. He spreads out the pasture, safe from predators and poisonous weeds, practically like a picnic before them; he examines and treats with oil their cuts and infections; he may even use his hands or his hat to make a cup for them to drink from when there is no quiet pool.

So with us; God is with us in the dark and dangerous places. If you sent any kind of condolence to Mrs. Robert Kennedy, you probably received an acknowledgment in the form of a little black-bordered card on which were printed the words that her husband had spontaneously quoted when he himself had been informed of the assassination of Martin Luther King, Jr.:

> Aeschylus wrote: "In our sleep, pain that cannot forget falls drop by drop upon the heart and in our own despair, against our will, comes wisdom through the awful grace of God."

And on another card she put a favorite quotation of her own:

> Blessed are they who mourn: for they shall be comforted. Blessed are they who hunger and thirst after justice: for they shall be fulfilled. Blessed are the peacemakers: for they shall be called the Children of God. (Mt. 5:3, R-D)

The psalmist is nearly done. But he adds one more sentence:

> Surely goodness and mercy shall follow me
>   all the days of my life;
> and I shall dwell in the house of the Lord
>   for ever.

Strangely enough, the sentence is both overtranslated—
that is, it says more in English than it does in Hebrew—
and undertranslated. The Hebrew simply says, "as long
as I live" (JB). What he was talking about was frequent-
ing the Temple (the "house of the Lord") for his natural
lifetime. For all his spiritual genius and insight, the
truth of immortality had not been revealed to him any
more than the truth of relativity had been revealed to
Newton or moondust to Galileo. From our vantage point
we have a right, I think, to overtranslate it that way,
but we must admit that it is not what the psalmist had in
mind.

The undertranslation is in the word "follow." That is
too mild and placid a word. What the Hebrew means is
more like this: goodness and mercy shall *pursue* me every
day of my life. That too, as one old Scottish preacher
pointed out, is, or can be, a shepherd's figure.

One day in England on a narrow country road we
came upon a farmer moving his sheep from one pasture
to another. He had a helper in the form of a dog. The
intelligence and skill of a good sheep dog is proverbial,
and we had a chance to see a small example of it. Our
car—or something else—startled the sheep, and they
began to bolt in the wrong direction. But with no more
than a word, or a gesture at most, from the farmer, the
dog was off, fairly flying, and headed the leaders, turning
them to where they were supposed to go and saving them
from their own sheepish fear and stupidity. He didn't
follow them; he pursued them.

So it is with God's goodness and kindness—it does not
so much follow us as pursue us all our days. It is the sheep
dog by which he guides us and would save us from our
own folly. It is that "hound of heaven" of which Francis
Thompson wrote. Although it takes every generation a

long time to find it out, sex is not the essence of love; the essence of love is goodness and kindness.

You cannot outrun or outsmart goodness and kindness. You can betray it for thirty pieces of silver. You can give it a mockery of a trial in a kangaroo court. You can scourge it with a whip and crown it with thorns. You can wash your hands of it and nail it to a cross. You can laugh it to scorn and see it suffer and die. You can block its tomb with a great stone and post a guard. But it will rise again and be recognized by its own. It will appear when you least expect it and it will pursue you to whatever hell you make for yourself or for others. For goodness and mercy is God's own sheep dog—no, it is more: it is God's own self, his very nature, and will not let us go.

Chapter 10

THE BIBLE'S
MOST MISUNDERSTOOD
BOOK

THE MOST MISUNDERSTOOD BOOK in the Bible is The Revelation to John. It has been read and reread and misread so much that it is now often unread. Some have thought it was a crystal ball for foretelling the future history of the world. Some have seen in it a television spectacular, in color, of heaven. One of its cryptic figures of speech has been variously identified as Mohammed, the Pope, Napoleon, the Kaiser, Hitler, and Stalin; and there are doubtless those who now identify it with Mao Tse-tung or Chou En-lai. Largely on the basis of this book, people have calculated the end of the world at A.D. 380, 1000, 1030, 1715, 1734, 1769; it was widely believed in this country that the date was October 22, 1844; and as recently as 1959 a "sizable group from various parts of the country gathered at a farm near Waco, Texas" for the catastrophic end. And, on the other hand, there are those who have so misunderstood it as to believe that it is without any value at all for moderns:

Reasonable theologians (wrote the great German scholar Reimarus) prefer to refrain from the seven-sealed book and confess that of all its wonderful

visions they cannot with certainty interpret a single
one.[51]

If you have ever tried to read the book, you have some
idea why it is misunderstood! It almost seems to invite
misunderstanding. Native common sense is soon baffled
by its "weird world of fantasy, peopled with spectral
shapes and uncouth figures, where angels flit, eagles and
altars speak, a land where locusts have men's faces and
beasts have poisoned tails, and monsters rise from sea
and land." [52] It seems at times like nothing so much as a
clinical report of a nightmare shown in Cinerama. Its
strange language—the jargon of a man who thought in
Hebrew but wrote in Greek, apparently—is the despair
of translators. Even those who have spent scholarly lifetimes studying it will confess that there are parts of which
they cannot make head or tail. Ordinarily I recommend
that you read for yourself the passage I choose from the
Bible's "bunch of everlastings," but in this case I do not
unless you are prepared to make a thorough study under
competent leadership, unless you are willing to take time
for a patient and painstaking unraveling of mysteries
wrapped in enigmas.

I

Let me hasten to add, however, that all of us can
have a basic understanding of it and be saved from the
pitfalls which have snared so many. The very first word
of the book, in Greek, is *apocalypsis*. (It is the word
translated as "revelation.") And it is one of the chief
clues to understanding the book, for it identifies a particular form of literature.

When I say "poem" you think of a certain form of
literature, one with a certain meter, usually in rhyme.

When I say "novel" you think of a certain kind of literature, a story with a plot and characters written in prose. When I say "essay" you think of a certain form of literature, one in which a particular idea or proposition is expounded. And when we read "apocalypse" we should also think of a certain definite kind of literature.

There are two great examples of apocalyptic literature in the Bible. One is The Book of Daniel, the other The Revelation to John. There are several briefer examples of the same sort of thing, the most famous one being the thirteenth chapter of The Gospel According to Mark. But there are many more examples of this type of literature outside the Bible than in it. Jesus' life was largely lived in an apocalyptic framework; it was one of the most popular types of Jewish literature. It did for the people of that day almost what the newspaper, the historical novel, and science fiction all rolled into one do for us. It provided their understanding of history, a commentary on the present scene, and the popular notion of things to come.

Apocalypse is the literature of a people undergoing severe and unjust persecution. In Old Testament times that severe and unjust persecution of the Jews was furnished by the Greek empire, and The Book of Daniel is the classic result. In New Testament times the persecution of Christians by the Roman Empire had its classic result in the book of The Revelation to John. The historic background of Revelation is the generation from A.D. 64 to 93: the years from the time that Nero blamed the burning of Rome on the Christians and inflamed popular hatred against them to such a degree that Christians were impaled on sticks, smeared with pitch, and set on fire (as well as being beheaded and crucified in the normal manner), to the rule of the cruel, morose, suspicious, and probably insane Domitian, who thought he was himself divine, demanded that all his subjects worship him as a god and carried on a fierce persecution of Christians. John, the author, was himself a prisoner in a Roman concentration camp on the island of Patmos (Rev. 1:9) when he wrote at least part of the book. Apocalypse is the literature of people in a time of crisis.

One of the characteristics of apocalyptic literature— as meter is one of the characteristics of poetry, or plot is one of the characteristics of the novel—is to speak in symbols, in images, in sign language. It also commonly speaks with a double meaning, so that if it falls into the hands of the oppressors, it will seem harmless. Roland Hayes, whose grandfather and father were slaves, says that the origin of the Negro spiritual "Steal Away to Jesus" was something like this: it would be sung when there was going to be a secret meeting of the slaves at a prearranged place, but the white masters hearing it thought only of it as a harmless religious song. It was a kind of apocalyptic.

Still another characteristic of apocalyptic literature is the use of fantastic word pictures. Revelation has been called an "inspired picture book"; a friend of mine came closer, I think, when he compared its fantastic descriptions to editorial cartoons. Cartoons often personify impersonal objects; they often have grotesque exaggerations; they make free use of mythical figures; they bring together strangely incongruous elements and their meaning is crystal clear only to those who already have in mind some background information, usually from current events or from history. A Rip van Winkle who had slept through the last thirty years, for example, would probably find most editorial-page cartoons published this morning hard to understand.

Knowing these characteristics of apocalyptic literature, then, we are neither surprised, dismayed, nor betrayed into wild guessing games when we find Revelation to be full of images, unnatural monsters, and double-talk. Knowing that it was written for Christians with a crisis on their hands—the pagan Roman Empire—we will not frantically look for some crisis of our own age to explain it.

John, however, though speaking directly to and for his own generation, under the inspiration of the Holy Spirit did it in such a way that all generations since have been able to profit from his work. Exercised upon an issue of life and death, laboring under profound religious conviction, his intuitive genius and deep mystical piety gave classic expression to some truths of everlasting value to all ages and generations.

I

The book plainly divides itself into two parts, the first of which consists of seven short letters addressed to seven Christian churches in Asia Minor—just across the channel to the mainland from the island where John was a political prisoner. They are letters that have an amazingly contemporary ring and their arrangement characterizes the basic kinds of Christians now as then.

First of all, John says, *there are some Christians who make Christ sick*. The shocking boldness of that somewhat revolting phraseology is not mine; it is his. He says literally that Christ is going to vomit them out of his mouth. They nauseate him.

Who are they? They are the ones symbolized by the letters to Ephesus (Rev. 2:1–7) and to Laodicea (ch. 3:14–22). Ephesus was the most important city in Asia

Minor; Laodicea was a proud and wealthy city. But John says no word against the importance or the pride or the wealth of the towns these Christians live in. Is it, then, that the Christians there are believing the wrong things? There are always those who think that doctrinal purity is the most important thing. If it weren't so sad, it would be funny how separate Christian churches have been established over such beliefs as whether a candidate for baptism should be immersed forward or backward. But John specifically mentions that those at Ephesus have successfully spotted false apostles (Rev. 2:2) and have rejected the free-and-easy doctrines of the Nicolaitans (v. 6); so it is not theological heresy or unorthodoxy that is the trouble.

What then? Are they shirkers? Are they the ones who always let someone else do it? That type of person rates pretty far down on my own list. It is a commonplace that in a church, a union, a political party, or anything else, only a fraction of the members do most of the work. But no, bad as that is, that is not their trouble. John knows their "toil" (Rev. 2:2); they have prospered in worldly goods (ch. 3:17), and you don't usually do that without work. The people he is talking about are not freeloaders.

The thing that makes Christ sick about these church members is their lukewarmness (ch. 3:16); their enthusiasm is tempered, their radiation is carefully controlled to a low level, they have lost the love they once had (ch. 2:4). They are comfortably complacent: "For you say, I am rich, I have prospered, and I need nothing" (ch. 3:17). They are respectable and affluent middle-of-the-roaders.

A few years ago *The Christian Science Monitor* quoted an article that had appeared in a Red Chinese magazine.

The article stated flatly that Communists cannot share any kind of human relationship with non-Communists, even in one's own family. When you become a member of the Party in China, it maintained, you cease to be a member of any other group not affiliated with the Party; you belong to it body and soul. Young Chinese away from home in work camps, it said, who complain of homesickness, are guilty of "a bourgeois sentiment that has no place in the new society." That is pretty strong stuff; most of us instinctively resist it. But it is no stronger than the claim that Christ lays upon us: "If any one comes to me and does not hate his own father and mother and wife and children and brothers and sisters, yes, and even his own life, he cannot be my disciple" (Luke 14:26). That is pretty strong stuff too! There is a kind of all-outness, an absoluteness of commitment, at the heart of Christianity that for the most part we ignore. If someone says that he would like to come to church but can't on account of business, we think little of it. Of course a man's business comes first. If a woman says she cannot pledge because her husband isn't a member, we understand. Of course one's husband comes first. If a person cannot do something because he is going to do something with his family, we agree that the family comes first. And we have a pretty consistent way of saying that we want peace, but defending our own nation of course comes first. Ah! The lukewarm Christians are the ones who make Christ sick.

Now, secondly, John says in these seven letters that *there are some Christians who please Christ.* He symbolizes them, also, in two churches—the ones at Smyrna and Philadelphia.

Again, they are not the ones whom we might first think of. They are not the ones with the finest church building, nor do they have the largest budget for world service and benevolence. They are not the ones with the best public relations, the most eloquent minister, or the finest choir. In fact, they are not at all well thought of in their own communities. They live in poverty; the most religious people in town scorn and slander them (Rev. 2:9); they have but little power (ch. 3:8). When one stops to think of how closely that description parallels those living in the inner city today it is enough to make one pause! These are the people in the first-century world who were the most loyal, faithful, and pleasing to Christ!

But the point is that there were then some people worthy of the name of Christian, and the same thing is true now. We sometimes forget that. Seeing so much of hatred, bitterness, and meanness in the world, we forget that there are people who aren't that way. One of the radio stations in my town has taken to having one of its daily news broadcasts devoted exclusively to good news. I think that is a good idea; the spotlight is on the corruption, the tragedies, the accidents, and the wars more than enough. Do you remember that scene in which the Old Testament prophet Elijah is moping in a cave? Although he had struck a notable blow for righteousness, his spirits were depressed; he was tired of the uphill fight against corruption in high places. He had seen the crowd follow the bunkshooters again and again. He was sure that the nation had forgotten its religious obligations and rejected its proper leaders; he went so far in his private inner conversation with God as to say, "I, even I only, am left; and they seek my life, to take it away" (I Kings 19:10). God was not to be found in the fierce destructiveness of the wind or in the earthquake or the fire. But then there comes a "still, small voice" to tell him that there are seven thousand Israelites, tried and true, who have not sold out. It was true. And it is true now. There are Christians whose fidelity is pleasing to Christ.

Here is this vastly complex cancer of racism. There is more than enough idiocy being practiced on all hands. I know that. But there is sometimes a surprisingly large amount of sanity being practiced too. My hat is off to the young Negro athletes who were willing to sacrifice personal ambitions and risk missing a once-in-a-lifetime chance at the Olympics in a nonviolent exercise of power. My hat is off, too, to Archie Moore who used to be the light-heavyweight boxing champion. He is proving to be in as good mental condition as he ever was physically. He is stalking and counterpunching the problem in his own way.

> I was born in a ghetto, but I refused to stay there. I am a Negro and proud to be one. I am also an American and I'm proud of that. . . . I am a staunch advocate of the Negro revolution for the good of mankind. I despised the whites who cheated me, but I used that feeling to make me push on. . . . The Negro still has a long way to go to gain a fair shake with the white man in this country. But I believe this: if we resort to lawlessness, the only thing we can hope for is civil war, untold bloodshed and the end of our dreams. . . . Something must be done to reach the Negroes and whites in the ghettos of this country, and I propose to do something. I have been running a program which I call ABC—Any Boy Can—teaching our youth, black, white, yellow and red, what dignity is, what self-respect is, what honor is. . . . If some bigot can misguide, then I can guide. I've spent too much of

my life building what I've got, to put it to the torch just to satisfy some ancient hatred of a man who beat my grandfather.[53]

I do not know whether Archie Moore officially has his name on the book of any church in the country, but I would hazard the guess that he is one of the people who is pleasing Christ today.

Then John says that *there are Christians about whom Christ has mixed emotions.* They make him weep sometimes and they make him rejoice sometimes. And John seems to imply that there are more of these Christians than either of the other kinds, by a ratio of three to two—they are found in the churches at Pergamum, Thyatira, and Sardis. They have been faithful for the most part but a little casual in their acceptance of pagan ideas and practices (Rev. 2:14–15), they are something less than uncompromising in their attitudes (v. 20), and they have a good name but aren't really as good as they look (ch. 3:1).

Years ago Kermit Eby was the executive secretary of the Chicago Teachers Union. One day an indignant mother came into his office. She launched into a tirade against the Kelly-Nash political machine which then ran Chicago. The examinations for teachers were a farce, she said; if you knew the right people, you could have the paper "fixed." The superintendent, she went on, was just a tool of the politicians; the whole system was riddled with graft and rotten with corruption. Eby had been fighting the situation for years and he couldn't have agreed more with her than he did. But before he could say anything she went on to say that she had a daughter whose grades weren't good enough to get into Teachers College and asked him to recommend a politician who could get her in! Eby later wrote: "I think I understood her dilemma, but I also saw the political accommodation on which Lincoln Steffens said all political corruption rests. We want honest cops and honest judges, but we also want our tickets fixed." [54]

Ah, who among us has not "chipped the edge of the cube of truth" in order to make it roll a little? Who among us has not compromised a conviction here in order to gain a little advantage there? Who among us has not decided that something we knew to be going on was not really our business?

This is the message of John's seven letters: there are some Christians who make Christ sick, there are some who please him, and there are some about whom he has mixed emotions. It is as true now as it was then.

II

The second part of The Revelation to John is longer and harder to understand. But with patience and imagination we can at least understand the main message, even if some of the details are so strange and foreign to us as to be undecipherable. One of its timeless teachings is *the certainty of the ultimate triumph of good over evil.* This is a message common to all apocalyptic literature: after evil has done its worst, good will come out on top. The beasts and other horrible figures of Revelation are all embodiments of evil. And they all go to ultimate, final, complete destruction before Christ, who is the embodiment of good.

A delegation of bank presidents once urged Abraham Lincoln to give up all thought of saving the Union. However wrong slavery might be, however enduring the Union was meant to be, better to let the slave states go, they said. The President told a story in reply. "When I was a young man in Illinois," he said, "I boarded for a time with the deacon of the Presbyterian church. One night I was roused from my sleep by a rap at the door, and I heard the deacon's voice exclaiming, 'Arise, Abraham! The Day of Judgment has come!' I sprang from my bed and rushed to my window, and saw stars falling in great showers; but, looking back of them in the heavens, I saw the grand old constellations, with which I was so well acquainted, fixed and true in their places. Gentlemen, the world did not come to an end then, nor will the Union now." [55] Well, that's the sort of calm, invincible assurance that Revelation breathes. Behind the tumult and catastrophe and brutal injustice of his day John saw God standing within the shadows keeping watch above his own. He was confident of the ultimate triumph of good over evil.

Another everlasting truth of Revelation is that *allegiance to God is above allegiance to one's nation.* In ordinary times and under normal circumstances Christians have taken the view of the apostle Paul, "the powers that be are ordained of God" (Rom. 13:1, KJV)—that a Christian is a law-abiding citizen (cf. I Peter 2:13–17; 3:13) with obedient respect for civil authority. But Christians have also always held that at some times and under extraordinary circumstances we are called to "obey God rather than men" (Acts 5:29). One of the earliest incidents in the life of the church was a case of outright civil disobedience by Peter and John (Acts, chs. 4; 5), and, as historian Roland Bainton once put it, "if it had not been for three centuries of uninterrupted civil disobedience there would have been no Christian Church." Civil disobedience was not invented by Thoreau nor by Mahatma Gandhi nor by Martin Luther King; it is part of the legacy of Revelation. It was civil disobedience that first got John into trouble with Rome and then incarcerated on Patmos. He would not worship the emperor as divine and he exhorted his fellows not to worship the emperor either. Worship, he held, belongs to God alone (Rev. 22:9); idolatry is idolatry even when in the guise of civil law. So, many a Christian suffered and died for putting his allegiance to God above his allegiance to his empire.

It is hardly any more popular in our time to do that than it was in John's. Many American Christians have their doubts about supporting Christians who have disobeyed laws designed to enforce racial segregation for fear of encouraging lawbreaking and anarchy. Many have advised no one to participate in nor encourage civil disobedience, because such things "only encourage juvenile riots" and "contribute to the breakdown of law and order."

But a Christian not only will break the letter to preserve the spirit of a law, he will break a lower law to keep a higher one. He will evaluate both the letter and the spirit of civil law in the light of moral law; if they do not jibe, he will be obedient to the moral law, knowing that he will have to pay whatever penalty the civil law may lay upon him. This is what John urges his readers to do.

A Christian will break a law to draw attention to inhumanity and injustice if there seems to be no other way of effectively working to change such a law. Again, he will be ready to pay the legal penalty but hopes that by so doing he will appeal effectively to the slumbering consciences of the majority, who alone can change the law.

The unequivocal Christian position is that our alle-

giance to God is above our allegiance to the nation. "My
country, right or wrong," is the creed of the pagan. "My
country, under God," is the creed of the Christian.

One more everlasting thing Revelation says is that
there are times when *we serve best in God's cause by
patient endurance, by unswerving loyalty to Christian
conviction.* Again and again we read, "here is a call for
the endurance . . . of the saints" (Rev. 13:10, etc.). That
is a much-needed lesson for us, for we are activists, we
like the head-on approach that produces immediate results. Back at the turn of the century, Rev. Charles
Henry Parkhurst was battling against the corruption of
the Tammany machine in New York. He discovered that
not only were the full forces of evil arrayed against him
but also a good many solid citizens looked askance at
his reforming zeal. They quoted the Bible to him: "The
wicked flee when no man pursueth." "Lay off this
politics," they urged. The next Sunday, the doughty war-
rior gave out as his text, "The wicked flee when no
man pursueth,' but he maketh a lot better time when
somebody chaseth him!" That's our American temper,
and it has its place. But the warfare of the Kingdom isn't
primarily a blitzkrieg; it's a long, drawn-out battle of
attrition. The tremendous, tenacious, inveterate power
in evil is only slowly worn away by the steady dripping
of dedicated life upon it (as we see in the Africa of
Schweitzer and Carlson); its massive, granitic strength is
often best split asunder by the growing roots of moral
lives. We won't see the final defeat of evil, no matter how
we strive; but all of us can contribute to its final overthrow by patient endurance, by personal integrity, by unswerving loyalty to Christian convictions. "The Apocalypse is a call to arms, but the arms are only patience

and loyalty to conviction." [56] *Revelation is almost a text-book in nonviolence.*

So we have come to the end of our survey of some books of the Bible, and I close with an incident from one of our own country's times of crisis. During the Battle of Bull Run a northern woman saw the disastrous rout of the Union Army. Washington, D. C., was almost in panic for months. All that she believed in and lived for seemed in danger of imminent destruction. From her hotel she could see the campfires of the Confederate Army. Later, visiting the troops, she wrote a poem, which has become a hymn, and rightly so, because it breathes the faith of Revelation and of the whole Bible:

> Mine eyes have seen the glory of the coming
> of the Lord;
> He is trampling out the vintage where the
> grapes of wrath are stored;
> He hath loosed the fateful lightning of his
> terrible, swift sword;
> His truth is marching on.

NOTES

1. Robert Gordis, *Koheleth—the Man and his World* (The Jewish Theological Seminary of America, 1951), p. 122.

2. Roland H. Bainton, *Erasmus of Christendom* (Charles Scribner's Sons, 1969), pp. 280 f.

3. Woody Hayes, quoted in *Sports Illustrated,* Sept. 24, 1962, p. 130.

4. Woody Hayes, quoted in *Time* magazine, Dec. 6, 1968, p. 65.

5. Bainton, *op. cit.,* p. 174.

6. Michael Novak, quoted in *Time* magazine, Dec. 5, 1969, p. 27.

7. William Sloane Coffin, *The Christian Century,* Nov. 12, 1969, p. 1449.

8. Gordis, *op. cit.,* p. 3.

9. Henry Fielding, *The History of Tom Jones: A Foundling* (The Modern Library, Random House, Inc., 1943), p. 690.

10. I have not been able to determine the author of this rhyme, which was given to me by word of mouth.

11. Herman Melville, *Moby Dick or, The Whale.*

12. James J. Kavanaugh, in a letter to the editor, *Time* magazine, Dec. 6, 1968, p. 19.

13. Winston Churchill, *The World Crisis, 1911–1914* (London: Thornton-Butterworth, 1923), pp. 68 f.

14. Francis Gerald Ensley, *John Wesley Evangelist* (Tidings, 1955), p. 51.

15. John Bartlett, *Familiar Quotations* (Little, Brown & Co., 13th ed., 1955), p. 422.

16. From "Epitaph," in *Collected Poems,* by Thomas Hardy (The Macmillan Company, 1925; 10th printing, 1964), p. 657.

17. Erica Anderson, *The Schweitzer Album* (Harper & Row, Publishers, Inc., 1965), p. 158.

18. S. R. Driver, *An Introduction to the Literature of the Old Testament* (Charles Scribner's Sons, 1902), p. 79.

19. Quoted in *Time* magazine, Sept. 5, 1969, p. 58.

20. *Ibid.*

21. Quoted in the bulletin of the First Methodist Church of Eugene, Ore., Dec. 29, 1957. No source given.

22. Quoted by T. P. Ferris in a sermon on May 15, 1960; published by Trinity Church, Boston, pp. 1 f.

23. First stanza of "The Hound of Heaven," by Francis Thompson.

24. Anne Morrow Lindbergh, *Gift from the Sea* (Pantheon Books, Inc., 1955), pp. 114 f.

25. John Steinbeck, *East of Eden* (The Viking Press, 1952; 5th printing, 1961), p. 413.

26. Robert H. Pfeiffer, *Introduction to the Old Testament,* 2d ed. (Harper & Brothers, 1941), p. 471.

27. *Ibid.,* p. 474.

28. Herman Wouk, *This Is My God* (Doubleday & Company, Inc., 1959), p. 51.

29. Quoted in *Life* magazine, Vol. 19, No. 8 (Aug. 20, 1945), p. 32.

30. American Friends Service Committee report, *Peace in Vietnam* (1966), pp. 76 f.

31. Quoted by Darrel Berg in a sermon on Sept. 24, 1967; published by Trinity Methodist Church, Lincoln, Nebr., p. 1.

32. In *A Compend of Wesley's Theology,* ed. by Robert Burtner and Robert E. Chiles (Abingdon Press, 1954), p. 26.

33. F. Gerald Ensley in a sermon on Nov. 24, 1940; published by the United Church of Norwood, Mass., p. 10.

34. T. P. Ferris, in a sermon on Aug. 8, 1954; published by The National Radio Pulpit (National Council of the Churches of Christ), p. 18. Used by permission.

35. Quoted in Gerald Kennedy, *A Reader's Notebook* (Harper & Brothers, 1953), pp. 176 f.

36. Albert Schweitzer, *The Quest of the Historical Jesus,* tr. by W. Montgomery (The Macmillan Company, 1954), p. 403.

37. F. Gerald Ensley, in a sermon on Jan. 14, 1951; published by the North Broadway Methodist Church, Columbus, Ohio, p. 9.

38. Rudyard Kipling, *Rewards and Fairies* (Doubleday & Company, Inc., 1910).

39. Phillips Brooks, 1868.

40. Bonaro W. Overstreet in her book *Hands Laid Upon the Wind* (W. W. Norton & Company, Inc., 1955).

41. M. K. Gandhi, *Gandhi's Autobiography: The Story of My Experiments with Truth,* tr. by Mahadev Desai (Public Affairs Press, 1948), p. 8.

42. Kipling, *op. cit.*

43. Edward Sanford Martin, "My Name Is Legion," in *Masterpieces of Religious Verse,* ed. James Dalton Morrison (Harper & Brothers, 1948) p. 274.

44. Carl Rogers, *On Becoming a Person* (The Riverside Press, 1961), pp. 107 f.

45. Anton Boisen, *Out of the Depths* (Willett, Clark & Company, 1950), pp. 196, 201 f.

46. Fran Tarkenton, *Sports Illustrated,* July 31, 1967, p. 42.

47. Lecture at Columbia University, quoted by T. P.

Ferris in a sermon on Dec. 10, 1950; published by Trinity Church, p. 6.

48. A. J. Cronin, *Adventures in Two Worlds* (McGraw-Hill Book Company, Inc., 1952), p. 320.

49. Martin Luther King, Jr., *Stride Toward Freedom: The Montgomery Story* (Harper & Brothers, 1960), pp. 137–138.

50. Ann Landers' newspaper column, published in the *Oregon Journal,* March 17, 1970, Sec. 2, p. 2.

51. R. H. Charles, *Studies in the Apocalypse* 2d ed. (Edinburgh: T. & T. Clark, 1915), p. 46.

52. James Moffatt, in *The Expositor's Greek Testament,* ed. W. Robertson Nicoll (George H. Doran Co., 1897), Vol. V, p. 301.

53. Archie Moore, *Sports Illustrated,* Aug. 21, 1967, p. 9.

54. In *The Christian Century,* March 15, 1950, p. 156.

55. *Lincoln's Own Stories,* collected and edited by Anthony Gross (Garden City Publishing Company, 1926), p. 184.

56. Moffatt, *op. cit.,* p. 313.

Index of Biblical References